WHERE DO
I BELONG?

AN IMMIGRANT'S
QUEST FOR IDENTITY

By: Tony Mankus

D1512231

To Lilija —

Thank you for attending the plaubuk

Regards,

Tony Martin
4/01/2015

INTRODUCTION

Everyone has a story, they say. This one is mine—at least the immigrant part of it. It's not remarkable, as some stories go—not like the one about the rock climber who cut off his arm in order to save his life, for example; but it's an honest accounting of a part of my life.

I wrote it because I couldn't afford a shrink, I like to say—only partly in jest. I started it years ago as an effort to deal with the imbalance I felt inside of me. I couldn't quite put my finger on it, but I knew it had to do with my past. Getting therapy would've been the usual way to deal with it, except that I couldn't afford it. Even if I could've, I didn't feel comfortable about therapy.

So I decided to start writing about my past. I began with the early years of my life, which were still vivid in my mind. Some of the events were painful to remember and I had to stop from time to time, sometimes for days or weeks on end. But I always went back to it, sooner or later.

As I made progress, I began to feel better about myself. I also started to do research about the bigger events surrounding my personal experiences, which helped to put them into context. That's when it registered with me that I wasn't alone; that my experiences, or very similar ones, were shared by many thousands, even millions of other people—and some of theirs were much worse than mine. So I decided to turn my writing into a memoir. I thought it could be a part of our family history, as well as a sharing experience for those of us who have felt a sense of displacement, alienation, and a need to find ourselves.

I wrote about some events simply because they were so vivid in my mind. I hope they help to illustrate the larger themes of the memoir: displacement, loss of identity, immigration, and trying to make it in a new environment.

Regarding the research material included in the book, I didn't cite the sources because this memoir is not intended to be a scholarly work. Much of it came from the myriad websites on the Internet, including Wikipedia, and I hereby acknowledge my gratitude to the authors. The relatively recent inventions and development of the personal computer, the Internet, and the search engines like Google, have made knowledge incredibly accessible and more widely available than at any time in the history of the world.

I also wish to express my thanks to the remaining members of my original family who have contributed to this memoir with their recollections. They include my brothers John and Ray and my sister Maria.

DEDICATION

I dedicate this memoir to my mother and father—God rest their souls. They led a hard life. I also thank God for my health and strong spirit. They helped me to survive and better myself.

TABLE OF CONTENTS

Chapter 1:   World War II...1

Chapter 2:   Exodus..5

Chapter 3:   Refuge During the War 13

Chapter 4:   Post-War Germany 25

Chapter 5:   Life in the DP Camp...35

Chapter 6:   A Glimmer of Hope...47

Chapter 7:   Trip to America...57

Chapter 8:   Elizabeth, New Jersey 63

Chapter 9:   The New and the Old..75

Chapter 10:   Teen Years 83

Chapter 11:   Kelly's Poolroom 95

Chapter 12:   Chicago 105

Chapter 13:   The Real World..121

Chapter 14:   Who Am I? 133

Chapter 15:   The Last Straw 145

Chapter 16:   Fairleigh Dickinson University 155

Chapter 17:   Peace Corps 169

Chapter 18:   IRS – Newark...189

Chapter 19:   IRS – OIO 199

Chapter 20:   IRS – Puerto Rico...221

Chapter 21:   IRS – Chicago 229

Chapter 22:   Home Sweet Home 239

Appendix i

The Mariachi Mass in the Cathedral of Cuernavaca...................i

Big Sky Country... xv

Muisne xvii

CHAPTER 1

WORLD WAR II

I remember hearing the guns. They were the heavy ones. When they went off, I could feel them on my eardrums, on my skin, in my bones— and they were becoming louder by the hour. I was only five at the time and didn't know what to make of them. The low booms sounded like thunder, the only sound I could compare them to.

Mom barked out edgy orders to us kids. We became hyperactive and ran around playing rough games that usually involved knocking each other over. The dog ran under a kitchen chair every time cannon fired.

Dad called everyone into the dining room. Unlike most of the other rooms, it was kept clean and uncluttered. The stained wooden floor and the large Blaupunkt radio Dad loved to listen to, lent an air of dignity to it. We gathered around him in a circle and fell silent; we even stopped fidgeting.

"Those are Russian cannons," he said. "They're firing at the German soldiers that are retreating back to Germany. The Russian army is chasing them and will be coming through our town again."

We waited silently while Dad paused to think. I didn't understand everything he was saying, but I sensed it was serious.

"Some of you may be too young to remember," he began again, "but the last Russian occupation was pretty bad. A lot of our people were shipped off to Siberia in cattle cars and most of them didn't come back. We have to decide what we're going to do."

There was silence again. We didn't know what to say. Mom was the first to speak, tears welling in her eyes. "I don't want to go," she said. "Our home is here." She wiped her eyes with the apron.

"We may not be so lucky this time," Dad responded.

"But where will we go?" Mom pleaded. "What will happen to us?"

"Trains are heading to Germany with the retreating soldiers," Dad said. "We can get on one of them. Raudys said he wants to go, too."

Raudys was our neighbor and a friend of Dad's. A lot of other people were leaving, too. Dad decided to go. The bottom line was that he didn't want to find out what another Russian occupation would be like.

The Soviet tanks reached Plungé, our small town in the northwestern part of Lithuania, on October 8, 1944. We left maybe a day or two ahead of them. We took only what was needed for the next few days: food, some clothing and blankets, and what little else we could carry. The rest had to be left behind.

Mom cried again. It's not hard to imagine why: the life she and Dad had worked so hard to build would be gone, possibly forever. There would be no trace of it left, other than the memories. What the future held—or even if there was to be a future—was unknowable. She kissed good-bye her beloved cow, the one that had provided milk to us children, and left.

A steam-driven locomotive pulled the train we boarded. The water in the large tank was heated by coal. The diesel engines being developed around that time hadn't found their way into Lithuania yet. When the conductor shifted into gear, the pistons chug-chugged the steam out the chimney and the train began to gain momentum.

We kids were excited. It was going to be a new adventure. I don't think that was the feeling among the adults, though. I saw Dad gazing out the boxcar door. Maybe he was saying good-bye. As it turned out, he and Mom would never see Plungé—or Lithuania—ever again.

Going to Germany was a risky proposition. The Russian armies were heading west toward Germany; the Western Allies had landed in Normandy on D-Day in June 1944 and were fighting their way east, squeezing the German soldiers in the vise of the two armies. In retrospect, it seems like we were jumping out of the frying pan and into the fire. But I'm not sure we had too many options at the time, or knew what they were.

So at age five I became a war refugee, a displaced person. I didn't realize then that being displaced from your land of birth is more than just a physical dislocation; it's also a disconnect from your identity. After we left Lithuania, the feeling of not really belonging anywhere didn't go away for a long time.

CHAPTER 2
EXODUS

We climbed into a boxcar with our belongings and made ourselves as comfortable as we could. Besides Mom and Dad, our immediate family included my two older brothers, John and Ray, ages twelve and eight; and my ten-month-old brother, Henry. Our extended family included my great aunt Diode; my maternal grandmother, Domincėlė, who was about sixty at the time; my Mom's sister Eva; and her seven-year-old daughter, my cousin Irene.

We were joined in the boxcar by Raudys, who brought his wife and young daughter, the only family he had at the time.

It was October and the nights were getting cold. There was no heat in the boxcar, of course, although we kept the sliding door partly open to let in some fresh air. My little brother Henry was bundled up in the baby carriage that we managed to bring for him.

As the train rolled on through the night, the carriage moved back and forth slowly, depending on the incline of the terrain. No one paid much attention to it since the land in that part of Lithuania was flat. Before long, everyone fell asleep. We were all worn out from the stress and uncertainty of the last few days.

I was the first to wake up early the next morning, just as the sun was rising. I looked around and noticed the carriage. It was very close to the open door. I sensed danger, but was afraid to say anything. The strange surroundings and the confusing events of the last few days had shut my usually chatty mouth. Fortunately for Henry, Raudys woke up at that moment. He jumped out of his makeshift bed on the floor and yanked the carriage back. "Wake up everyone!" he shouted out with nervous energy. "Who left the baby carriage so close to the door? Henry almost fell out!"

Everybody jumped up suddenly and began to level accusations at each other when they realized what had happened.

"I told you to push the carriage up against the wall," Dad barked at Mom.

"Diode was the last one with him," Mom retorted.

Diode usually got the blame for everything. She didn't defend herself. She just shuffled over to the carriage in her nightclothes and tucked the blanket around the baby.

I felt guilty too. "I woke up first," I said, trying to get someone's attention. "I saw the carriage close to the door. I should've pulled it back. I'm sorry."

The adults were too agitated to pay attention to me. Those who heard me didn't take me seriously. Maybe they thought I was just trying to boost my sense of self-importance. Raudys made a half-hearted effort to scold me, but I'm not sure he believed me either.

I crawled back into my makeshift bed on the floor and thought about the day Henry was born. My two brothers and I were alone in the house with our cousin Irene, waiting for the adults to come back from the hospital. We made up a game we called "train," which meant we had to crawl on our hands and knees under all the chairs arranged around the dining room table, as if we were the cars of a long train. "Toot, toot," I intoned.

When we got tired of playing train, we took turns counting to see who could count the highest. "One million," I announced, certain that I would top everyone.

"One hundred zillion," Ray chimed in before I could bask in my victory.

Then all the adults came home. Dad was carrying a bundle wrapped in a white, frilly blanket. Mom seemed pale and weak, although her eyes sparkled when she saw us kids lined up to watch the goings on. Diode, our great aunt, helped Mom to remove her winter coat while Eva, my mother's sister, took the bundle from Dad. I was curious to see what was in the bundle.

Dad announced with a twinkle in his eyes that he had a present for us. He said it was "stinky," though, and that Aunt Eva was going to change it. Then the bundle began to cry. I sort of figured out it was a baby, but I couldn't understand what all the excitement was about.

I approached Aunt Eva cautiously to have a closer look. Aunt Eva was a widow, for all practical purposes. She didn't know whether her husband was still alive. He'd been shipped off to Siberia during the first Soviet occupation, a few years after they were married. She never heard from him again. My cousin Irene was their only child. Since there was no man to look after them, Aunt Eva and her daughter cast their lot with our family, more or less. It was a symbiotic relationship, based as much on need as on love and affection. She wasn't overly fond of my father, though, because of his hard drinking.

"This is your little brother Henry," she said quietly as I peered into the small opening of the bundle. His eyes were closed, although his mouth seemed to be making some sort of contortions. *Maybe he's trying to tell me something*, I thought. I didn't realize at the time that his mouth was just contorting in some reflexive way and that there was no significance to it. In retrospect, though, I wonder sometimes whether he *was* trying to tell me something—like some idiot savant, maybe—about the future that would end so sadly for him.

Later that afternoon, the train lurched to a stop. We heard an airplane buzzing overhead, diving at us with the staccato fire of machine guns. We jumped out of the boxcar and dove into a ditch along the track. One of the passengers was hit in the leg before the plane flew off.

Fortunately, that was the extent of the casualties. We were lucky the plane didn't have any heavier ordnance, such as bombs. We got back on the train and resumed the journey.

After a few days, we stopped in Breslau, a Polish city near what used to be the Czechoslovakian and German borders, although it historically was a source of border conflicts between Germany, Czechoslovakia, and Poland. We had to change trains before we could go on through Czechoslovakia on our way to Germany.

As we waited in the train station, German soldiers, some with rifles and submachine guns slung over their shoulders, barged in. One soldier, with a Luger in his right hand, was in front of the others. He scanned the room to see what was going on. The waiting room fell silent. Everyone looked away in an effort to be inconspicuous. Mom squeezed me closer to her while Diode held on tightly to Henry. John and Ray sat by Dad and stopped fidgeting, sensing the tension in the room.

The soldier with the Luger spotted John, my twelve-year-old brother, and walked over to him. "You!" he barked in German. "You come with us."

Mom cried out in grief, but Dad hushed her up. John hesitated, unsure of what to do. He looked at Dad who was squeezing Mom's hand, trying to calm her.

"*Schnell! Schnell!* The German officer barked again, waiving his pistol for John to follow.

John stood up and followed the soldiers. He threw a quick glance back at us once before he was led out of the room. He wasn't crying, but you could tell from his blazing eyes that he was scared. Mom began to shake, sobbing with grief.

John was taken to a local *Hitlerjugend* school in Breslau where he attended classes in math and Nazi ideology, among other things, and was required to pass tests of physical strength. He was presented with the *Blut und Ehre* dagger for passing the athletic feats he was tested on. John doesn't remember many of the details. Maybe he was so frightened during captivity that he blocked out most of those memories. He does remember an older woman, though, the math teacher, and her strident voice. She taught them the multiplication table by repeating the numbers in German—over and over again—until they had memorized the answers correctly.

It's not clear why John was kidnapped, but it's likely that he was caught up in the Nazi *Lebensborn* program, which was begun in 1941 for children born of selected Nazi men and women. Hitler's vision was to swell the Aryan population with a form of genetic engineering. The program was later expanded to include kidnapped blond, blue-eyed children from other European nationalities. They were given new German names and placed in institutions, or fostered with families that had pledged to bring them up as good Germans. At this stage of the war, though, the teen-age boys also underwent rigorous physical training at the *Hitlerjugend* schools in order to prepare them to become good Nazi soldiers. Due to the heavy casualties of the war, the Germans armies on the home front were filled with young boys and old men.

John did what he was told, but for the two or three weeks he was held captive, he plotted secretly to escape. One night, when everyone had settled down for the night, he sneaked out of the school and scurried back to the train station to look for us. He approached a family that he overheard speaking Lithuanian and asked if they had seen us.

"What's your name?' the man asked John.

"Jonas, Jonas Monkevičius," John answered.

"No, I'm sorry. I don't know anybody by that name."

We were long gone by then, of course, and no one knew where. John stood there silently, not knowing what to do. The man was preoccupied with the survival of his own family, but felt sorry for this forlorn boy.

"We're getting on this next train," he said, trying to be helpful. "It's going to Germany."

John stood there, undecided. He didn't know whether he'd find us in Germany, but he didn't want to go back to the *Hitlerjugend* school. "Many of the families that left Lithuania are heading there," the man said.

Not having anything else to go on, John decided to do the same. He climbed up and positioned himself between the cars. He was afraid to sit inside for fear of being questioned and sent back to Breslau as a deserter.

As the train rolled on, he became numb from the cold. It was November already. He wore only light clothing; he had been afraid to put on his overcoat when he left the school for fear of being noticed.

John shivered and fought the urge to fall asleep. He was old enough to know that if he fell asleep, he'd tumble down under the wheels of the train and meet a certain end. Even though John blocked out many of the memories from this episode, he remembers vividly to this day the overwhelmingly numbing cold and the deathly fear of falling under the wheels.

But John's survival instinct must've kicked in and he managed to hang on for a day or two, until the train arrived at the outskirts of Kempten, Allgäu, a Bavarian town in the southern part of Germany. Apparently this was the train's destination, so he climbed off and just started walking along the tracks. Then—incredibly—he spotted Mom and us kids and ran stumbling toward us.

CHAPTER 3
REFUGE DURING THE WAR

John joined us where we had set up shelter in some railroad cars. They were on a spur off the main tracks, as best as I can remember. Maybe they were deactivated and that's why no officials seemed to bother us. In addition, organization in Germany was starting to fall apart in the latter stages of the war. The Germans were more concerned about their personal survival than about chasing off war refugees from deactivated railroad cars.

The passenger car we occupied had wooden seats and iron-grill storage racks running along the upper part of the walls. There were no beds, no kitchen appliances, no heat, and no bathrooms. We managed to make do, though. By early spring, it got warm enough so that heat wasn't a big problem. Bathrooms weren't essential; the outdoors served as our commode. The lack of a kitchen was a moot issue: there was no food.

Dad, John and Ray went on regular outings to forage for food. They started by looking to see what they could find nearby. The train cars that arrived regularly were a logical target. They'd break the seals of the cars and plunder them for any canned or packaged goods, keeping an eye out for German soldiers.

At one of the outings they noticed a warehouse nearby and ventured there to look for food. As they got closer, they spotted several corpses, just torsos with no arms, legs, or heads. Maybe they were victims of land mines or bombs, although Dad didn't stop to investigate. He and the boys tiptoed gingerly around the corpses and entered the warehouse where they found sacks of potatoes. Notwithstanding the shock of the dead bodies, this was lucky booty they were able to bring back to our makeshift shelter.

After a while, they had to expand their range to nearby farmhouses. At one of the stops, they encountered a young German woman who lived on a small farm with her infant daughter. She seemed sympathetic, considering the circumstances, and took pity on us. She gave us bread, eggs and milk, whatever she could spare.

She was a widow, we found out. Her husband had perished in Stalingrad. He'd never seen his daughter who was born after he'd gone off to war. My parents carried a picture of her and her only daughter for many years thereafter. I don't remember the woman's name, but I'm grateful that she saved us from starvation.

She didn't always have enough food to share with us, though. By late 1944 and early 1945, the German economy was in shambles and food was scarce, even for someone who could afford to buy it. When the weather turned warmer in the spring of 1945, we'd hike to the nearby woods where we gathered berries, mushrooms and nuts. That was our last resort.

On one particularly bad day, when the food was almost gone, Dad gathered everyone into a circle again. Whenever he did this, we knew it was something serious. We stood apart from him and gave him some space. In this moment of crisis, everyone knew that, for better or worse, he was the head of the family.

Dad was thirty-six at the time, in the prime of his life. He was handsome and strong. He loved order and clarity. He thought that the difference between right and wrong was unambiguous; pretty much black and white. He didn't acknowledge gray. He thought you could achieve anything through honest, hard work, especially work that required strength and the use of your hands. He set high standards for himself and for us kids. He thrashed us from time to time for disobeying him, or for not living up to his standards.

The problem was, though, he couldn't always live up to his own standards. His outlet was drinking—binge drinking. Once he started, he didn't want to stop. At times, this would go on for days.

At any rate, Dad announced that spring morning that all we had left was less than a half loaf of bread. "I'm going to split it up amongst us, as best as I can," he said. "I'm sorry. That's all we have. I won't take any myself."

He broke the half loaf into smaller pieces and handed them out. I wolfed mine down in a second; I hadn't eaten since the day before, when I had an equally sparse meal.

"I'm still hungry," I said, feeling empty and sad. Tears welled up in my eyes, and I began to cry. I felt so down that I couldn't help myself. Everyone looked at me quietly. No one knew what to say. Finally my brother John gave me his piece. "Here," he said, handing it to me roughly. "And shut up already."

A little later, he threw up. It must've been from the digestive acids that were eating away at the lining of his stomach.

Although I was still hungry, I felt a little better. Maybe I was mollified by my brother's sacrifice. I went off to the side by myself and thought about the christening party we'd had for Henry only a few months before. We'd had lots of food then.

I remembered Dad preparing for the party by slaughtering a pig. He went into the pen with a big knife. Mom, Diode, and we kids came out to watch. I remember vividly to this day the details of the scene that followed.

The pig sensed danger and started making nervous grunts. It paced the dirt floor in short spurts, turning rapidly one way, then the other. Dad set the knife down on the ground, spit in the palm of his hand, and rubbed it against the other—a sure sign he meant to get down to business. There was a glint of focus in his eyes as he crept closer to the pig, backing it into a corner of the pen. The pig became more agitated and paced even more nervously.

Dad opened his arms wider, getting closer with each step. The path that the pig paced became shorter and shorter. The grunting became incessant and higher-pitched. When Dad got close enough, he lunged for the pig, but it squealed and scooted out of his grasp, kicking furiously with its hind legs. Dad's arm was scraped in the exchange and blood began to ooze through the skin.

Mom and we kids let out a groan. Mom shouted out instructions to Dad, telling him how to trap the pig. "You're giving it too much room," she yelled. "Get closer before you lunge for it."

The glint in Dad's eyes became brighter. His face took on an expression of grim determination. The pig had drawn first blood; there was no turning back now. The hunt was on and wouldn't end until there was a kill.

Dad's adrenaline kicked in, sharpening his reflexes. With the next lunge, he grabbed the pig around the middle and lifted it to his chest with his powerful arms. The pig squealed with amazing volume and pitch. I covered my ears to muffle the loud shrieks of terror.

Dad carried the pig over to where the large knife lay on the ground. He picked it up with his right hand while he encircled the pig firmly with his left arm. He placed the large knife against the pig's throat, as if to mark the spot, and then slashed it with one sweeping motion.

Blood gushed out of the open gash. For a second, the pig's squealing stopped. The silence felt eerie. Then the squealing and the squirming started again. But the pig's strength began to ebb almost immediately. The squealing and kicking became weaker with each gush of blood. Dad carried it over to the bucket Mom had placed in the pen and let the blood drain into it. It would be used for soup and sausages.

After the pig died, Dad disemboweled it and singed the outer layer of skin over an open fire to burn the bristles. The air was pungent with the smell of burning bristles and skin. He then turned the pig over to Mom, Diode, and Aunt Eva. They washed it, cleaned it thoroughly, and roasted it over an open spit.

That Sunday evening, we had a feast. We ate sausages, *kugelis*, and *cepelinai*. I watched Mom prepare all of the dishes with the help of Aunt Eva and Diode. To make *kugelis*, Mom peeled and grated a bunch of potatoes into a slush that she poured into a large, rectangular pan. She added eggs, bacon, seasonings, and other ingredients to the mixture and then baked it in the oven. When it was done, it had a spongy texture inside and a crust on top. It was delicious.

The *cepelinai* were also made from grated potatoes which were shaped to look like little footballs, or miniature zeppelins—as in the helium-filled dirigibles invented by Count Ferdinand von Zeppelin. That's how Lithuanians got the name *cepelinai*, an idiomatic conversion of the word Zeppelin.

Before boiling them, Mom filled them with meatballs about the size of golf balls. That was the fun part eating the *cepelinai*: you found the little meatballs inside.

After the christening ceremony in church, everyone gathered in the dining room: Mom, Dad, Raudys, Aunt Eva, and several other friends and neighbors, together with their children. Dad broke out *Krupnikas*, a homemade whiskey of grain alcohol, honey, and herbs.

A raucous party ensued. The men sang the traditional drinking song in a polka tempo:

> *Kad vis teip būt, kad vis teip būt,*
> *Kad visos dienos šventos būt,*
> *Kad viena diena dirbama*
> *Ir ta pati geriama.*

Loosely translated, it means that it should always be that all days are holidays; that one day, and one alone, should be a working day; and that even that one should be a "drinking day."

The women served the food, laughed along with the men, and made half-hearted efforts to control the kids. The kids ran around, reveling in the general excitement and festive atmosphere. John and Ray took advantage of the loose supervision. They got under the dining room table to smoke cigarette butts that had been dropped carelessly to the floor and to drink some of the *Krupnikas*. I just sat next to Mom, eating *kugelis* and *cepelinai*.

But those moments were only a memory now. Memory was a good way to escape reality, but it only lasted for so long. Hunger and other unpleasant things, like bombing, had a way of bringing you back to the present.

Since we were on the railroad tracks, we were targets of regular Allied bombings. In the spring of 1945, they became more frequent and intense. On warm, sunny days, we tried to avoid them by hiking to the nearby forest. Those outings, as we called them, offered relative safety from the bombings, as well as some nourishment. We usually spent the day picking berries and mushrooms. They were pleasant interludes in an otherwise dreary situation. If the weather wasn't good, though, we'd seek safety in the underground bomb shelter nearby as soon the sirens sounded.

During a particularly heavy bombing raid, we huddled in the cold and damp air raid shelter as bombs exploded above us. Some exploded in the distance, while others were much closer. The ones right above us exploded with sudden and shuddering impact. They jarred our inner ears and left our bones trembling with reverberations of the aftershock. I clung to Mom, afraid to move, or even breathe.

The sound and physical impact of those explosions were more powerful than anything I'd ever experienced in my short life. They were more powerful and frightening than the loudest cracks of thunder I'd ever heard in the middle of a summer night. Mom couldn't make up a story to explain them like she could explain the claps of thunder. She didn't even try. All she could do was wrap her arms tightly around Henry and me.

After a while, the bombing stopped. The shelter was silent. Even though it was filled with dozens of people, all I could hear was the heavy breathing of my Mom and the rapid beat of my heart. Everyone waited for the next teeth-shattering explosion.

When none came, people began to stir.

Dad was the first to speak up. "It seems to have stopped," he said. "I think I'll go up the stairs to see if it's safe."

"Don't go up yet," Mom warned him. "Wait a little longer."

But Dad wouldn't be deterred. He had a sense of bravado about him—something he had adopted after surviving his harsh youth, I imagine. Dad was placed at an early age into the servitude of a man who owned a large estate. I guess his mother wasn't able to care for him. She was probably too poor. I'm not sure. I never knew much about him, or his parents, for that matter. Dad never talked about his family—at least not to us kids. Every time we broached the subject with him, it was clear from his grunts that he didn't want to talk about it.

The name of the landowner was Vladislovas ("Vladas") Komaras, and his estate was in the village of Baisogala. I do remember hearing Dad and Mom talk several times about Komaras and the village of Baisogala, which was, and still is, a small village of two or three thousand inhabitants. The village was largely agricultural when Mom and Dad lived there, though it also had some small commercial establishments owned and operated by Jewish merchants.

Historical references to the town date to the thirteenth century. The name Baisogala is a combination of two words: *baisus* and *galas*. Together, they mean "a terrible end." There are several theories about the origin of the name. One is that during the wars with Viking invaders, the native defenders had a saying that the Vikings would meet "a terrible end." Another theory is that some centuries ago, a wooden road was built to facilitate commerce between several larger towns in the area. It ran through the village of Baisogala, which was surrounded by dense forests. Merchants would often be attacked and robbed on the Baisogala stretch of the road, so they named the town "a terrible end."

Vladas Komaras's family had owned more than a thousand hectares of land going back to 1830. After Lithuania gained independence from Russia in 1918, the Lithuanian Seimas (Congress) passed land-reform statutes in 1922, and Komaras lost all but eighty hectares. After the first Russian occupation of Lithuania in 1940, he was arrested. He died in captivity a year later and his eighty hectares were turned into a Soviet-style collective farm.

But when Dad lived and worked there, Komaras still was a powerful landowner. Dad worked in Kormaras's swine husbandry enterprise. I guess the women who worked there probably took care of him—if you could call it that. They were probably too busy with their work and with their own children to care for him properly.

At the age of five, or so, he was sent to school, but he didn't last there very long. After a half year he dropped out. Very likely, economics was one of the main issues. So Dad was put in charge of caring for farm animals on the Komaras estate. He fed them, cleaned the pens, and slaughtered them when Komaras gave the order. The work made him tough and self-sufficient.

So anyway, back in the bomb shelter, Dad climbed up the clay stairs cautiously after the bombing stopped. He pushed the door open slightly and peeked out. At that moment, a bomb went off. Maybe it was one that had failed to detonate on impact. The air compression slammed the shelter door shut and hurled Dad down the entire flight of stairs, a distance of twenty or thirty feet.

Fortunately, he wasn't hurt. There were no structures or hard edges inside the shelter, only damp clay. He stood up quickly with a nervous laugh. "I'm OK," he said wiping a wet spot on his clothing. "I'm not hurt."

When we climbed out of the shelter, it was dusk. The setting sun cast long shadows across the enormous destruction around us. Particularly eerie to me were the railroad tracks. Many of them had curled up into semicircles with the open ends pointing toward the sky, almost like praying figures raising their hands to God. I tried to imagine the enormous power—perhaps it was the searing heat of the explosions—that could cause iron beams too heavy for ten men to curl into such suppliant shapes.

If there was no warning before the bombs started to fall, we'd dive under the bench seats of the railroad car and pray that there would be no direct hits. One time, Diode had just helped Henry to go potty into a pan when explosions started. Mom shouted for everyone to dive under the benches. But Diode got so nervous and confused that all she could do was run back and forth in the train car carrying the fully loaded potty pan. With the gallows humor that my parents later developed about the war, they had a lot of laughs about that incident—at Diode's expense, of course.

One spring morning in 1945, it was sunny and pleasantly balmy and Mom let me out to get some fresh air. I was playing on the railroad tracks when, out of nowhere, a fighter plane appeared in the cloudless blue sky and started spraying machine gun bullets at me. They piff-piffed off the dirt and pinged off the railroad ties before ricocheting at acute angles. Hearing the staccato machine gun and the angry buzz of the diving airplane, Mom rushed out and screamed, "Run under the railroad car! *Now!*"

I was too confused to know what was going on, but the sound of Mom's desperate voice was enough to make me dive for safety. The pilot probably couldn't tell I was a child. Maybe he was just emptying the left-over bullets on his way back from a sortie.

After a while, all bombing stopped. We heard rumors that the war was ending. Sometime in June 1945, a young American soldier from a detachment of the First US Army strolled into our makeshift refugee compound. He was dressed in a GI uniform with a helmet and carried an M-1 rifle. He couldn't have been more than eighteen. He looked suspiciously at us. The war was just winding down and there still were German soldiers and snipers, as well as hostile civilians around. He wasn't sure if we were friendly or not.

Dad put on his big smile and waved. He couldn't speak any English yet, but having lived through several occupations of Lithuania, he'd learned to communicate in a histrionic way. He had Mom retrieve a few chocolate bars that we'd pilfered from one of the train cars and offered them to the young soldier. In exchange, the soldier offered Dad a cigarette. Dad took it and lit his and the soldier's in the traditional, male bonding ritual.

After a few puffs, the soldier relaxed and decided to show off his marksmanship. He picked up a German soldier's helmet that was lying next to the railroad track and placed it on a mound of dirt in front of the concrete wall of the bomb shelter. He turned and paced away from the helmet in large steps, counting as he did so. When he reached the count of fifty (we counted along with him in Lithuanian), he faced his target, positioned himself on the ground, aimed carefully, and fired several rounds. The second one hit its mark. The helmet jumped off the mound and rolled over.

We all walked back to the helmet and examined it. It had a gash in the front, where a German soldier's forehead would've been. Dad smiled and shook the GI's hand in a ceremonial gesture. My brother John was impressed. He began to ask the soldier to identify objects in English, starting with the rifle and the helmet. Then he repeated the words to the soldier's approval.

I looked at the young soldier with awe and wonder. Somehow, in some intuitive way, the terror of the bombs, the zinging of bullets, the power of the forces that had uprooted hundreds of thousands of people and that had turned my young world upside down became just a little clearer to me. The conqueror of the mighty German military machine now had a face—a boy's face.

CHAPTER 4
POST-WAR GERMANY

After the war ended, Kempten, Allgäu, was in shambles. Although I remember some of the smaller details around us, I was too young to understand the larger picture. My subsequent research confirmed what I later imagined: buildings, homes, roads, bridges, and railroad tracks had been destroyed or heavily damaged. Food was scarce; injury and illnesses were rampant. Medical help and medicines were virtually nonexistent. And Kempten, Allgäu, was but a microcosm of the larger picture in Germany and other parts of the world affected by World War II.

The German government—what there was of it—was weak and barely organized, unable to help its citizens, much less the multitude of homeless refugees within its borders. Statistics were hard to come by during the early summer of 1945, but, according to some estimates, millions of refugees from different countries were on the move in Germany and in other parts of Europe under the control of the Western Allies. Millions more were migrating in Russia's areas of control in Central and Eastern Europe. Russia and the Western Allies had released close to eight million German soldiers who had been held as prisoners during the war. Those who hadn't been captured or injured and were relatively healthy simply laid down their arms and joined the movement of humanity trekking toward some destination.

This mass migration of peoples must have seemed like a surreal scene from one of Hieronymus Bosch's paintings. Men, women, and children of all ages and nationalities—Cossacks, French, Croats, Ukrainians, Germans, Poles, Silesians, Lithuanians, Belgians—dressed in rags, were packed tightly in dilapidated wagons, tanks, oxcarts, carriages, automobiles, trucks, and vans. They moved on muddy and rutted roads, heading for what was left of their homes, or at least looking for temporary shelters. Alan Moorehead, an Allied journalist, wrote:

> *Half the nationalities of Europe were on the march, all moving blindly westward along the roads, feeling their way by some common instinct toward the British and American lines in the hope of finding food and shelter and transportation there.*

The conditions of these refugees ranged from grim to unspeakable. They were dazed, disoriented, sick, and hungry. One American reporter, who was in Europe right after the war, saw a horse collapse and fall to the side of the clogged roadway. The driver got off the wagon the horse had been pulling, quickly removed the harness, and cut the animal's throat with a knife. As if on cue, other refugees swarmed the horse with their own knives and cut off hunks of meat while the horse was still alive. In less than an hour, all that remained of the horse were its skeleton and its head.

Many, like the Jews, were still housed in concentration camps where they had been held during the war. They were too sick or emaciated to move. When the Allied soldiers arrived at the Bergen-Belsen camp, they found at least fifty thousand prisoners inside, most of them seriously ill. Another ten thousand lay dead in huts or about the camp. Richard Dempley, a BBC reporter who'd accompanied the British soldiers, wrote this account of his visit to the camp:

> *Here over an acre of ground lay dead and dying people. You could not see which was which...The living lay with their heads against the corpses and around them moved the awful, ghostly procession of emaciated, aimless people, with nothing to do and with no hope of life, unable to move out of your way, unable to look at the terrible sights around them...Babies had been born here, tiny wizened things that could not live...A mother, driven mad, screamed at a British sentry to give her milk for her child, and thrust the tiny mite into his arms, then ran off, crying terribly. He opened the bundle and found the baby had been dead for days.*

After British and Canadian troops liberated the camp on April 15, 1945, they forced the remaining SS troops to bury the dead bodies. Over the next days, the survivors were deloused and moved to a nearby German Panzer army camp, which was renamed the Bergen-Belsen DP camp. The original Bergen-Belsen concentration camp was then burned to the ground with flamethrowers because of a typhus epidemic and louse infestation.

Other sites held slave laborers, mostly Polish and Russian prisoners of war, although they also included men and women of other nationalities. By some estimates, at least one million Polish and up to five million Russian prisoners of war were compelled by the Germans to work as slave laborers during the war. One such slave labor camp was the Wehrmacht tank casern near Neustadt. About 2,500 men and women, mostly Russians, were forced to work there. When the Allies came across the site in April 1945, they couldn't believe the chaos, debris, and filth they encountered. Bernard Warach, a Team I welfare officer with United Nations Relief and Rehabilitation Administration (UNRRA), reported that the prisoners had defecated all over the camp and there were incredible scenes of men and women fornicating in the dorms. After being kept apart by the Germans, they rushed together after the collapse of German control in an instinctive reaffirmation of life amid the death and squalor of the camp. All the UNRRA workers could do initially was just walk around, talk to the remaining survivors, and hand out C rations, the standard-issue GI food packages.

The occupation forces had to deal with the aftermath of the war. Control and command of the occupation forces in northwest Europe at this time was vested in the Supreme Headquarters, Allied Expeditionary Force (SHAEF), which was headed by General Dwight D. Eisenhower. One of SHAEF's first post-war priorities was to organize and classify this mass of displaced humanity and provide food, temporary shelter, clothing, and medical care until people could be repatriated to their countries of origin. Later, refugees were helped by civilian personnel from UNRRA, which eventually took over the entire operation.

Initially, the Allied soldiers organized Displaced Persons (DP) camps wherever war refugees were to be found, including numerous places in

Germany, Austria, and Italy. A DP camp was established for us refugees in Kempten, not far from our makeshift home on the railroad tracks. We moved to the camp as soon as it opened. They gave us a room and a kitchenette of sorts in a large, five-story stucco building, one of many in an orderly complex of such buildings constructed around a square. In all likelihood, it had previously been a military garrison, known in Germany as a *lager*. It was to be our home for the next five years.

The seven in our family shared this modest space with another family. Dad hung a few blankets from the ceiling in an effort to provide some privacy, though that was minimal at best. Eventually we got several rooms to ourselves as families moved out, or were repatriated.

I remember first hearing the term "DP" from an American soldier there. A lit cigarette dangled from the soldier's partly open mouth as he interviewed Dad. The smoke rose up from the tip of it in a thin, elegant line into his right eye, making him squint while he tried to focus on the manual Underwood typewriter.

"D…P," he said, pronouncing each letter slowly as he clumsily poked the keys with his right index finger.

Dad stood in front of the soldier, waiting respectfully to answer the questions that were posed to him through an interpreter. The soldier rolled the paper forward and took it out. He placed another page in, took the cigarette out of his mouth, and broke the column of ashes into a coffee cup that served as an ashtray.

I was only six at the time and didn't remember hearing the term before.

"What does DP mean?" I asked Dad.

"Displaced Person," he said, "but they call us DPs for short."

"What's a Displaced Person?" I asked him.

"A war refugee," he said. "People like us who had to leave their homes and their land because of the fighting."

I knew we'd left our home in Lithuania because of the war, but I didn't understand how the term "DP" described us. The soldier didn't know anything about us or what happened to us during the war, and he didn't seem to care; he just wanted to process the paperwork that had to be done and move on to the next refugee family.

The soldier put the cigarette back in his mouth and continued filling out the questionnaire. He asked Dad for his date of birth, his marital status, the number of children in the family, his country of origin, his education, etc. This information was later used to create new documents in place of the ones we didn't have with us, such as birth certificates. I still have a notarized translation of a birth certificate created for me at the DP camp on August 23, 1948. It apparently was based on church records from Plungé. It appears that the Western Allies were able to gain access to some of those records in Lithuania before the Iron Curtain came down for good.

The Allied soldiers did their best to administer to our needs. Additional help arrived later through UNRRA. We were grateful for any assistance, regardless of what they called us. The plan was to repatriate us to our countries of origin as soon as possible in order to relieve the immense logistical burden of caring for the mass of displaced, sick, and malnourished humanity. Many left as soon as they were able to, following medical authorization. Others, however, like most Poles, Ukrainians, and other Eastern Europeans, didn't want to be repatriated because of the Russian occupation.

The Russians tried to persuade SHAEF to repatriate us Lithuanians because we were Soviet citizens. We balked at that. We'd had a taste of what it was like to be an involuntary Soviet citizen and didn't want to be reunited with "Mother Russia." Fortunately for us, Kempten was in the western sector of Germany, which was under the control of Americans and other Western Allies. After a while, they became sympathetic to our argument against repatriation and allowed us to remain in the DP camps for the time being.

The refugees in the eastern sector of Germany didn't do as well. They were sent back to their countries of origin, now occupied by the Soviets, under a deal worked out, more or less, between US President Franklin D. Roosevelt, Soviet General Secretary Joseph Stalin, and UK Prime Minister Winston Churchill at the Yalta conference, when Roosevelt was already very sick and near death. Of course, the deal worked out at the Yalta conference required free elections in countries under the "protectorate" of the Soviet Union, but that never happened. It took the repatriated peoples almost fifty years to regain their freedom from the Soviet Union—if they survived that long.

We Lithuanians in the DP camp in Kempten managed to organize ourselves somewhat. Organization was essential not only for the logistics involved in survival, but as a reaffirmation of our identity. In her book, *DP*, Milda Danys, a Canadian historian, wrote that having lost their self-respect, property, careers, and power over their environment, and being entirely dependent on others' charity for their survival, the Lithuanian DPs could find meaning in their lives only in their national identity. "Being Lithuanian was a constant, and to this frail thread of identity Lithuanians clung."

Some of the more prominent and educated Lithuanian men were elected to be our representatives with the military and UNRRA authorities. One of the first things they did was to get authorization to organize a school for the kids. I remember looking over the shoulders of my older brothers, who'd already enrolled in the school. They brought home a textbook printed in Lithuanian. Besides the large lettering, it had pictures, which I liked. With the help of my parents, my brothers were trying to read their first assignment. I memorized every word they read. That served me well in my first day of school several weeks later.

Since I'd never been to school before, I thought this large gathering of kids my age was for playtime. I was busy being rowdy with the kids around me, paying no attention to what the teacher was saying.

"Children! Settle down, please!"

His calls for order were ignored.

"We have to begin class," he repeated. "Everyone, take your seats, please!"

When that didn't work, either, the teacher decided to make an example of me.

"Algis! Algis Monkevičius!" he called out. "Please read the first page of the book that you have with you."

The class fell silent suddenly and everyone turned to look at me. Finding myself trapped, I reacted instinctively and began to recite what I remembered from listening to my brothers read. In the meantime, I fumbled frantically with the pages of the book, trying to find the first chapter.

I doubt that I recited everything correctly, but it seemed to work. The children broke out into raucous laughter, apparently thinking I had outsmarted the teacher.

The teacher, who was also the principal of the school, looked at me in wonder. I doubt that I lived up to his expectations, though. My continued rowdiness disabused him of any hope he had for me. He was a kind and gentle man, however, and more patient with me and the other children than I would've been in that situation. I ran into him many years later at a cocktail party in Washington, D.C., and thanked him for putting up with me. He said he remembered me and my recitation of the first page from memory.

CHAPTER 5
LIFE IN THE DP CAMP

Studying wasn't what motivated me. Like most boys, I had lots of energy and just wanted to run around and play. I especially liked to play war games. In post-war Germany, that didn't take a lot of imagination. The military were all around, together with the military assets and ordnance, including guns, ammunition, jeeps, trucks, tanks, and airplanes. We could walk in the nearby woods and find rifles, machine guns, pistols, and rounds of live ammunition that had been abandoned by German soldiers. During one such outing, we were walking in a dry riverbed when I spotted a pistol stuck in the mud. I think it was a Luger. My brothers and the other boys had walked right by it without noticing it. I pried it loose and called out to them. "Hey, guys! Look at what I found!"

They rushed to examine it. They thought it was cool.

"Here, you'd better let me have it," one of the boys said, reaching for the pistol. I think he was envious that I had found it. "That's too dangerous for you."

"Yeah, you're too young for that," another one said. "I'm actually the oldest one here and I'd better take care of it."

I hesitated. I wasn't sure if I had a right to keep it. But then my brother Ray stepped in. "No," he said. "My brother found it and it belongs to him. He's got the right to keep it."

With that encouragement, I decided to take a stand. "Well, you guys can look at it," I said, "but I want it back. I found it and it belongs to me."

To my surprise, they gave in. That made me feel good, a little more grown up, maybe. It was the first time I caught on to the concept of ownership: something belonging to me. When I took the pistol home, though, I gave it to Dad, who turned it over to the authorities.

On that same outing, we gathered all the unspent bullets we could find. We stacked them in a large pile, put paper and dry sticks around them, and set them on fire. When the fire began to crackle, we ran off as fast as we could, keeping an ear out for the fireworks that were sure to follow.

Nothing happened. After a minute or two, we stopped and considered going back. Maybe the fire had gone out, we thought. As we started walking back, however, the bullets began to pop and we ran off to our next adventure.

Ray got the prize for the loudest and most dangerous incident we ever pulled off. Several days after our outing in the woods, he pried open dozens of bullets he'd brought back, took out the gunpowder, and poured it into a standard-issue, tin, army canteen. He then devised a fuse over the cap. One of the boys dared Ray to light it.

"C'mon, Ray, light it! Don't be chicken."

Ray wasn't chicken; a little crazy, maybe, but not chicken. As soon as he lit it, we all screamed at him to throw the live bomb. He flung it at the brick wall of a small tool shed nearby. The explosion demolished the wall.

Fortunately, no one was hurt. The loud bang caused a sensation in the camp, though. A group of adults ran over to see what had happened. When they realized it had been a prank, they forced us to reveal who was responsible. Even though Ray had done it, we all were punished.

Dad believed that it was his holy duty as a father to thrash us when we misbehaved. His thrashings were painful and humiliating rituals of biblical proportions. He thrashed us with the thick razor strop he used to sharpen his straight-edged razor. He made us pull down our pants and underwear and bend over. He then made us smell the thick belt before he lashed us with it, counting the lashes aloud. He usually decided how many lashes to administer before he began, though he might vary it depending on our reactions. If we showed anger or stubbornness, he'd increase the count. If we cried in genuine repentance, he might decrease it by a few. If he perceived that our crying was from pain alone, rather than from true repentance, the count wouldn't change.

Afterwards, he'd make us apologize for our transgression or misbehavior. Not infrequently, he or Mom would make us kiss his hand, the one that had just administered the thrashing.

After we got older, my brothers and I began to resist, or try to escape, Dad's thrashings. Wild scenes often followed. If we ran, Dad and/or Mom would chase us. Furniture, appliances, pots, and pans would be knocked over and we kids, or even our parents, would get bumps and bruises. If we were caught, Dad's lashes would have extra zest. If we bolted out the door, a thrashing was almost guaranteed to occur when we back—unless we were bold enough to stay away from the house long enough to make our parents worried. Then Mom would sometimes relent and send one of the other boys to find the escapee and tell him there'd be no thrashing if he came back. John was the only one bold enough to try that at the time. He was a teenager already and had some buddies who would give him food and let him sleep on the floor somewhere until things cooled off at the house.

I remember this one time diving under the bed, screaming in terror. I wasn't big enough or fast enough to escape. Dad pulled me out from under the bed by force, even though I held on to the bedpost with all my might.

As I got older, sometimes I'd refuse to cry, gritting my teeth to keep from making a sound. This only made Dad angrier and he would administer the lashes even harder. He usually won, though I did succeed on one occasion when I was close to ten. I held out from crying until Mom stepped in and made Dad stop. Maybe he wasn't angry enough to continue that day, or maybe he was just tired.

Mom often was an accomplice in these rituals, though sometimes she was a moderating influence, if you could call it that. If Dad's anger was too great, or if the thrashing was too severe, she'd step in and try to get Dad to stop. If Dad was too lathered up and refused to stop, she'd shout at him and even step in between him and the child in an effort to stop the blows.

In retrospect, this form of punishment was horrible and cruel. It separated me emotionally from my parents and from my own feelings. It took away my self-esteem and made it more difficult to interact meaningfully with other people.

Was I angry with my parents? You bet. But as I got older, I started to forgive them gradually. Although it took a long time, I came to terms with the fact that they were a product of their time, their culture, and their harsh upbringing.

So after the canteen explosion, Dad thrashed all three of us, starting with Ray. The next day when we went to the public showers, we received our second humiliation. All of the kids had heard about the explosion by the tool shed and laughed at the welts on our bodies. They thought it was funny.

Some of our pranks *were* funny, at least in retrospect. One day I sprinkled sneezing powder in a classroom filled with women who'd gathered for some sort of meeting. I was hesitant about doing it, but the other boys talked me into it. I tried to act nonchalant as I walked around, sprinkling the powder between the rows of seats. I must've put on a good act since the women didn't seem to pay much attention to me. Other kids about my age were in the room, too, and the women must've thought I belonged to one of the other moms.

After a minute of sprinkling, I left the room and walked out into the hallway. At that point, the sneezing began. A few of the women started, and then the sneezing spread throughout the entire room.

My fellow conspirators congratulated me and took off in a hurry. They didn't want to be around when somebody came out to investigate. I wasn't sure what to do next. I thought that maybe I should go in to see the sneezing women so that I could describe the details afterwards to my friends. That would score some points, I thought.

As I walked into the room, I saw dozens of women on their feet, sneezing uncontrollably. Between sneezes, they talked excitedly, trying to figure out what had happened. One of them looked at me suspiciously. She demanded to know whether I'd had anything to do with it.

"I'm sorry, ma'am," I said, looking at her with wide eyes. "I'm not sure what you mean." By now, I had perfected my "innocent boy" act. "What happened here, anyway?"

"Let me see your hands!" she demanded.

I showed her my hands. Fortunately, the powder didn't stain.

"Empty your pockets," she went on in an authoritarian manner. I did as I was told. Fortunately for me, my fellow instigators hadn't given me the whole box. If they had, I would've been convicted on the spot. I'm sure some of the shrewder women saw through my act. But, lacking any tangible evidence, they let me off with a tug on my earlobe and a slap on the behind.

Not all my pranks were harmless, though. One evening I sneaked out of our apartment. Mom was tied up with something and didn't notice my escape. I walked toward the buildings nearby and spotted some older boys, including my brothers, John and Ray. They were playing Ping-Pong in a wooden, one-story building. I tried to get in through the door, but it was locked. I called out, asking to be let in, but they ignored my pleas.

I looked around and noticed that one of the windows was broken. There was a jagged hole about the size of a grapefruit. Maybe someone had hit a baseball through it. I climbed up to the ledge, put my hand in through the hole, and opened the window from the inside. As I climbed in, I noticed blood dripping to the floor.

"Hey!" I shouted to everyone in the room, "Someone's bleeding."

That caught their attention. They stopped playing and turned to look at me. Then I looked at my hand and noticed that the someone was me. Blood was gushing out of my left hand. Apparently, I was so involved with trying to open the window while balancing on the ledge that I didn't realize I had cut myself. There was a nasty gash across the top of my hand and blood gushed out in spurts with each heartbeat. I got scared. One of the boys put a handkerchief over the cut, but it became soaked in seconds. I began to cry aloud.

"Who's that crying?" Mom shouted from the apartment window. Apparently, my crying was loud enough that she heard me.

John and Ray told me to be quiet. Fortunately for me, one of the older boys was a Boy Scout. He'd had first-aid training and realized that I had severed a main blood vessel and might bleed to death. He devised a tourniquet from another handkerchief and tied it around the upper part of my arm. That stopped the bleeding. He then led me and my brothers back to our apartment.

Mom took me to the infirmary right away. The doctor on duty asked me to move the fingers on my left hand and that's when I realized I couldn't move them. Apparently, I had also severed, or at least damaged, a tendon. I started to cry again. He then took off the tourniquet. When the blood began to gush out again, he called the hospital. I was admitted the same evening and had surgery early in the morning.

They wheeled me into the operating room. I was alone and scared. The room was cool and I shivered in the light hospital gown. The nurse told me she was going to put an anesthesia mask over my mouth. She told me to breathe deeply and instructed me to count to ten. Even though I felt a sense of foreboding about following her instructions, I did as she told me. Counting took my mind off my fear momentarily. The sweet but pungent smell of ether permeated my lungs and brain. Before I reached three, I was out.

When I awoke, I felt nauseous. The nurse brought a small pail and I vomited. Then I drank some water and felt a little better.

The days that followed were sad. No one came to see me, not even Mom. I guess she was too busy running the household. Maybe she had no transportation to get into town. I'm sure she had no money to come by taxi. Dad wasn't around; I wasn't sure where he was. Every day visitors came to see the man in the bed next to me. They brought him flowers, candy, and other presents. They talked in a lively manner and laughed a lot. I felt alone. I tried to keep from crying. I didn't want to seem like a sissy, especially in front of strangers, but I couldn't help myself. Tears ran down my cheeks.

When the visitors saw me crying, they came by my bed and tried to cheer me up. They spoke to me in German, but I couldn't understand them. We refugees kept pretty much to ourselves at the DP camp and spoke only Lithuanian. So the visitors tried to teach me some words in German. They pointed to an object in the room, like the bed, the window, and the lamp and encouraged me to repeat the words in German.

"*Das bett*," a woman said, pointing to my bed. She had a smile and seemed nice. Maybe she had a son or a daughter my age, I thought.

"*Das bett*," I repeated tentatively.

The woman and the others smiled and nodded their heads. I felt encouraged.

"*Das fenster*," the woman said pointing to the window.

"*Das fenster*," I repeated, a little more bravely. I was rewarded with additional smiles and nods.

In a few days, I began to understand them a little and even ventured to learn new words. They always encouraged me, although the conversations were limited. But I looked forward to their visits. There was no TV in those days and I had no games to play with or books to read. There were no other children my age in that wing of the hospital so I had no playmates. I needed something to take my mind off my injury and to stimulate my imagination.

Mom finally came on the day I was discharged. I was angry with her because no one had come to visit me for the ten days I was in the hospital. Even more upsetting was the fact that she didn't seem to notice my anger and didn't ask what was bothering me. I felt the urge to shout at her, *"Hey! Look at me! Look at what I'm feeling. I'm angry!* I finally mustered up some courage and blurted it out.

"How come no one came to visit me?" I asked, holding back the tears that were starting to well up in my eyes. I didn't want to seem like a sissy.

She looked at me with a mixture of surprise and embarrassment, as if I had touched a tender spot.

"The other patient had visitors every day," I continued, unable to hold back the tears any longer. "They came to see him every day and brought him presents. I was the only one who had no visitors."

She apologized and gave me a hug. "I'm sorry," she said. "I wish I could've come. I wanted to see you, but I couldn't get away. Dad isn't home and I had to care for your little sister. Will you forgive me?"

Her explanation and hug didn't take away the pain and the anger I felt. I wanted her to tell me more; tell me how much she missed me, how my friends were asking about me, and how glad she was that I was better and would be coming home. But she didn't say any of those things. I could feel that she didn't want to dwell on it. She changed the subject to getting me dressed.

"Come," she said, taking my clothes out of the armoire. "Let's get you dressed and bring you home. You'll be able to play with your brothers and your friends now. We'll be happy to have you home."

"Where's Dad?" I asked, pulling on my pants. "How come he's not home?"

Mom hesitated. She seemed even more uncomfortable. "He's away," she said.

I held off from asking any more questions. I found out later that Mom was at home alone with my three brothers, plus my sister, Maria, who had been born several months before. Although I knew Dad wasn't home, I didn't know that he was in prison. Apparently, he'd been convicted of manslaughter for killing a man while he was driving a military truck under the influence of alcohol. Even if I had known it at the time, I wouldn't have understood how shameful that was for Mom and how hard it was for her to try to run a household without a man's help.

As I started going through the mechanics of dressing, I began to see Mom, for the first time in my life, as a person separate and distinct from myself. Until then, I couldn't imagine not trusting her any more that I could imagine not trusting myself. But I couldn't put out of my mind the feeling of being alone.

Mom was about forty-two at the time. Like Dad, she was uneducated, although she could read and write. She had attended school for two and a half years before she was forced to pull out. She told us a number of times how much she had wanted to continue with her education when she was young, but that cost money—something her mother had little of. Her mother was a widow. Her father had died at age thirty-five, before Mom was born, leaving my grandmother pregnant and with two other children, Eva and Joseph, to raise.

Her dad, Kazimeras Gružauskas, was a descendant of the Gruževski (aka Gružecki) family from Poland. They settled in northern Lithuania in 1585 and became part of the landed nobility that included duchesses and a queen on one side of the family and members of Parliament and other high government officials on the other side. No one knew what happened to the land owned by Mom's father when he died in 1905. It might have been seized for debt, taken away by fraud, or forfeited to the government. Lithuania was under Russian occupation in those years and Russia was governed by the czar and his family.

All Mom knew was that they'd moved to the town of Baisogala after she was born, probably because there was a cousin there, a priest, who could offer some support. Mom begged her cousin to let her continue with school, but she was sent to work in a vegetable garden on the estate of Komaras, the same landowner in Baisogala where Dad worked. They were married in 1931, when she was twenty-five and Dad was twenty-two. Their wedding picture shows that she was a beautiful bride. In later years, she attributed her beauty and health, especially her perfectly formed teeth, to the vegetables she ate in that garden.

My outpatient treatment consisted of soaking the injured left hand in warm water several times a day and exercising it by repeatedly clenching my hand into a fist. For many years thereafter, I couldn't close the middle and ring fingers, or move them independently. Eventually, they became almost normal; I'm not sure the same could be said about my feelings of trust.

I did start to develop a softer side, though. There was a girl at school, a tiny blonde with pale skin. She was quiet, bashful, and very gentle. Her name was Rasa, which means dew in Lithuanian. I fell in puppy love with her and longed to be with her all the time. During school recesses,

I sought her out and wanted to play with her. After school, I offered to walk her home.

There was only one problem: she had another admirer. He was older and bigger than I was. I had to compete with him for her attention. Every time I tried to talk to her, this boy would step in between us and try to push me away. Sometimes this pushing would break out into a scuffle. I wasn't afraid of his size when it came to Rasa, though. I usually managed to hold my own. My passion for her more than made up for the difference in our sizes.

Sometimes he and I would try to outdo each other with feats of daring for her. One time, as Rasa watched, I climbed over the stair railing on the fifth floor of our apartment building and suspended myself from the ledge by one hand. The drop to the bottom of the stairwell was fifty or sixty feet.

"I bet you can't do *that!*" I shouted to the boy, making sure that Rasa was watching.

That was a feat the bigger boy didn't want to try.

She seemed to like me, although it irked me that she didn't tell the bigger boy to go away. I wanted her all to myself. But like all pretty girls, she'd already learned how to manipulate lovesick boys. She'd also learned, apparently, that passion can be heightened by competition. Eventually this love triangle broke up. She and her family left for America. I was sad to see her go. I asked her to write to me, but she never did. I thought I would never see her again.

CHAPTER 6
A GLIMMER OF HOPE

By 1949, most of the remaining families had begun to emigrate from Germany to other parts of the world, including Canada, Australia, South America, and the United States. Those countries had passed immigration laws to admit war refugees who couldn't be repatriated to their native lands, or didn't want to be, especially those occupied by the Soviet Union. The records show that Canada accepted 157,687 refugees; Australia, 182,159; United Kingdom, 86,000; Venezuela, 17,000; Brazil, 29,000; and Argentina, 33,000. President Truman signed the first DP act on June 25, 1948, which authorized the admission of 200,000 DPs from Europe. On June 16, 1950, he signed the second one, allowing the entry of an additional 200,000 refugees.

Although these immigration laws were great humanitarian gestures, they were not entirely altruistic. Many of the welcoming countries were experiencing rapid growth following World War II and needed cheap labor. The European refugees offered an ample supply to meet this demand. Australia was among the first nations to encourage immigration from post-war Europe. Besides its need for cheap labor, Australia also wanted to increase its population in general. Following its narrow escape in World War II, it was thought that the Japanese would have invaded Australia next if they hadn't been bombed into submission by the Americans. The fear was that Japan would have succeeded in conquering Australia because it did not have the population or the resources to defend itself properly.

Australia and the other countries began to compete for the younger and healthier refugees, as well as those from the more northern or whiter European nationalities. Although many of the European Jews met the white-European criterion, they weren't necessarily among the preferred immigrants. Historical prejudice against them lingered, and many were seen as "problematic."

Needless to say, the remaining European Jews had a different perspective. Having experienced atrocities before and during the war and watched their families, friends, and millions of their countrymen starved, worked to death, brutally tortured, or murdered, many felt dejected and pessimistic. Many saw Europe as a graveyard of their people and, for the most part, didn't even want to be repatriated to other countries. Dr. Samuel Gringauz, the head of the Jewish DP camp in Landsberg, Germany, expressed it this way:

> *We do not believe in progress, we do not believe in the 2,000-year-old Christian culture of the West, the culture that, for them, created the Statue of Liberty in New York and Westminster Abbey on the Thames, the wonder gardens of Versailles and the Uffizi and Pitti palaces in Florence, the Strassbourg Münster and the Cologne cathedral; but for us,*

the slaughters of the Crusades, the Spanish Inquisition, the blood bath of Khmielnicki, the pogroms of Russia, the gas chambers of Auschwitz and the massacres of entire Europe.

Some Jewish families tried repatriation to Poland, or to villages in Russia, but found anti-Semitism to be as strong after the war as before. Tens of thousands emigrated to America, or to other countries, as immigration became possible, but many more sought *Aliyah,* a permanent home. Increasingly, that home became Palestine, which was, more or less, the historical location where the Israelites had lived at various times from about the thirteenth century BCE, after the Exodus from Egypt, to around the seventh century CE, when Muslim Arabs conquered the region.

The roots of *Aliyah* go back to the first century BCE, after the Romans destroyed the second Jewish temple in Jerusalem in 70 CE, and enslaved the Jews. Those that could, dispersed throughout the world. Thereafter, the return to the Land of Israel remained a recurring theme among the generations of Diaspora Jews. Their prayers during Passover and Yom Kippur traditionally concluded with, "Next year in Jerusalem."

The problem was the Muslims and Arab-speaking peoples populated Jerusalem and the environs; there was no political "Land of Israel." The increasing influx of Jews in the twentieth century created tensions among the populace.

With support and encouragement of President Truman, the British, which had a mandate over Palestine after it had conquered it from the Ottomans in 1917, turned the issue over to the newly established United Nations. On September 1, 1947, the United Nations Special Committee on Palestine unanimously recommended that Britain give up its mandate on Palestine and partition it into separate Arab and Jewish states. This was approved by the UN General Assembly on the 29th of November, 1947.

The details of the UN resolution were never fully implemented, however. On May 14, May 1948, the day before the British Mandate was due to expire, Jewish leaders, headed by David Ben-Gurion, signed the Israeli Declaration of Independence. At that point, the tension between the Arabs and the Jews burst into open conflict. At first it was a civil war between Jewish Yishuv forces and Palestinian Arab forces, but turned into a war between sovereign states after an alliance of Arab states intervened.

Ironically, while the Jews finally attained their dream of *Aliyah*, it resulted in tensions and conflicts that continue to this day.

We Lithuanians lost our land to a brutal and tyrannical dictator and could not go back. The only saving grace for us—if you can call it that—is that we Lithuanians, as well as the other Baltic nationals, were considered less "problematic" and more welcome in other countries. Mom and Dad were still in their early forties and we were all relatively healthy. We were grateful for the opportunity to leave Germany—and anxious to get going.

We had one problem, though. My brother Ray couldn't pass his physical exam. X-rays showed that he had a spot on his lungs, possibly from tuberculosis. We had to wait until it cleared up.

The waiting was tedious. It had become very lonely in Kempten. The camp population had dwindled considerably and I had virtually no playmates. Rasa and her family had left for America and Ray Stadalnikas, my best friend in the camp, also had gone there with his family. Ray and his family settled in Hartford, Connecticut, I found out later.

When I was lonesome, I resorted to the one thing that was always there for me: daydreaming. I thought about my early years in Lithuania, the innocent years before I knew about what was going on in the bigger world. I thought about one sunny morning in April 1944 when the air had just turned balmy. It was shortly after my fifth birthday. A shaft of light from the rising sun angled in through an opening between the curtains in my bedroom and woke me up. I sat up and felt an urge to go out and play. Something told me that the long stretches of cold winter months were coming to an end. I wanted to smell the fresh air again, feel the blades of grass under my bare feet.

I tiptoed to Ray's bed to see if I could coax him into going out with me. He, and just about everyone else in the house, was still asleep—except for my Great-Aunt Diode, who was starting to stir the pots and pans in the kitchen. Her duties were the operational nitty-gritty of the household and she was getting ready to make breakfast for us.

"Wake up, Ray," I shook his shoulder tentatively. "Let's go out on the seesaw."

Ray turned his head away. He wasn't too happy about my intrusion into his deep slumber.

"C'mon, Ray," I persisted, shaking his shoulder again. "It's beautiful outside."

"Go away," Ray managed to mumble. "It's too early."

But I wouldn't go away. I kept shaking his shoulder until he stirred.

"You're a pain in the butt," he grumbled, sitting up slowly. He stretched his arms out and yawned with a slight shudder. He was eight already and had gotten used to my stubbornness.

"Just for a while," he said rubbing his eyes. "But I've got to get ready for school pretty soon."

He pulled on a pair of pants that had spent the night crumpled on the floor and we went into the backyard. He let me get on my end of the seesaw first before he climbed on his. I felt a rush of air on the upswing as Ray's weight whisked me up. He then pushed up with his legs and I zoomed down again. I let out a "whoop!" He was the engine and I was getting the free ride.

But then the fun stopped abruptly. On the next downswing, I stepped on a bee. It was crushed under my bare foot—but not before it stung me. The sudden jab took my breath away. My mouth opened, but no sound came out.

Ray stopped pushing off and looked at me in puzzlement. "What happened?" he asked.

I couldn't speak.

Ray got off the seesaw and let me down slowly. As he walked over to my side, the shock of the sting subsided into a focused pain and I let out a loud, prolonged wail. That woke up the whole household.

"What's going on!" Mom shouted, opening the bedroom window. "Ray, are you picking on your brother?"

"I didn't do anything!" Ray shot back defensively.

Mom came out, wrapping a bathrobe around her. "What happened, Algis?" she asked, approaching me. Her voice softened as she stroked my hair. "Is Ray being mean to you?"

I continued to cry, unable to speak. Mom turned to Ray, looking for some sort of explanation.

"Honest, I didn't do anything," Ray repeated. "We were on the seesaw and, all of the sudden, he just started crying."

Dressed in slacks and a white, sleeveless nightshirt, Dad ambled out the back door to investigate. "Are you guys getting into trouble again?"

he demanded, adjusting the tension in the suspenders. He wasn't in the mood for trouble so early in the morning.

"You," he said, pointing to Ray, "finish dressing and get going to school."

"You," he pointed to me. "Let's get you cleaned up and feed you some breakfast."

He helped me off the seesaw and started to walk me toward the house. As I took my first step, I went limp and let out another yelp.

"Here, let's take a look at that foot," Dad said, noticing my limp. His voice softened a bit. "Did you cut yourself?"

He sat me down on the back stairs and examined my foot carefully. Mom leaned over to get a closer look. Ray stopped his retreat and waited to see if the mystery was going to be solved. John, my oldest brother, came out of the house and joined the circle surrounding me.

"It looks like a bee sting," Dad announced. "That's not so bad."

Easy for you to say, I thought, continuing to cry.

"Here, let me see if I can squeeze it out," Dad said, hunching over to focus on my foot.

"No!" I shrieked, yanking my foot out of his hands.

"Be gentle," Mom urged Dad. "I'll go get some alcohol in the house."

"Get me some tweezers, too."

Dad took my foot in his hands. "Here, let me see what I can do."

I cried out again.

"It won't hurt. You'll see," he said, trying to reassure me.

I didn't believe him. I tried to yank my foot away again, but he hung on to it firmly. He was strong. He enveloped my tiny foot with his two large hands, put his two thumbs around the sting and squeezed.

I let out a scream.

"There," he said, pulling out a little black sliver with his forefinger and thumb. "It came out. That wasn't so bad, was it?"

He brought the tiny sliver closer to my eyes so I could see it. I tried to look at it, but the tears blurred my vision.

Dad picked me up and carried me into the house. He sat me down on a chair by the kitchen table. Mom brought over the alcohol and cleaned the bottom of my foot. I continued to snivel and cry half-heartedly, although the pain was starting to wane.

Ray and John left for school. Mom and Dad went off to work. I was left home with Diode and my younger brother, Henry. He was still a baby and fast asleep in his crib. All the noise I'd made didn't seem to bother him.

I continued to cry on and off, although it was less convincing—even to me.

"Well, isn't this silly of you to carry on like this," Aunt Diode said, bringing over some breakfast. It was potato pancakes and sausages—my favorite dish. I was tempted to eat.

"The pain is gone by now," she added, making believe she didn't notice me looking at the food. "Besides, no one is here to hear you anyway."

I'm not sure she convinced me the pain was gone, but she was right about the audience having left. I guess she didn't consider herself an audience. We kids never treated her that way. It just seemed like she was always around and we took her for granted. We kids "christened" her with the name Diode. It comes from the Lithuanian word *ciuoce*, which means aunt. But we couldn't pronounce it properly when we were young, so she became Diode.

Diode was about forty-five at the time and had never married. She was an old maid. Old maids didn't fare too well in those days. Either they became professional maids or they cast their lot with a family, as Diode had done, and became amateur maids. In return for food and shelter, Diode was expected to do whatever was necessary to run the household. She also received a measure of family affection, I guess, although that was a mixed bag, at best.

Her real name was Juozapata Palionytė. She was the sister of my grandmother on my mother's side. She fed us, bathed us, dressed us, picked up after us, wiped our behinds, and generally accepted whatever we took for granted without even a thank you. She rarely complained, although she sighed and grimaced a lot when she was tired. She also prayed a lot—at least whenever she found some quiet moments for herself. That wasn't too often. What with looking after us, cleaning the house, cooking, washing the dishes, doing the laundry, ironing, making the beds, and performing the countless other household tasks, she had little time for herself.

She usually prayed in the evenings, after everyone had settled down. Sometimes she would begin by looking at the gilt-edged picture of a saint she'd brought back from church. After contemplating it for a while, she'd turn it over and start "reading" the prayer on the back of it. She couldn't really read it, though; she was illiterate. But she'd "read" by repeating, in an audible voice, things she'd heard about the saint. After that, she prayed for health, for peace of mind, or for strength in her daily life.

More often than not, though, she'd just say the rosary. She'd sit on the corner of her bed reciting the Hail Mary and Our Father, over and over again, while she rocked gently back and forth.

I started to eat the potato pancakes. They tasted good. I raised my eyes to the window and gazed out into the yard. The sun was shining and the air was filled with the aroma of early spring. A few wild flowers swayed gently in the breeze. The only sounds that broke the silence were the chirping of birds and the occasional clanking of pots and pans as Diode cleaned up in the kitchen.

CHAPTER 7
TRIP TO AMERICA

Ray's tuberculosis finally cleared up by the summer of 1950. We were relieved and anxious to leave the DP life behind us. Dad gathered all of us into the traditional family circle to decide on which country we should go to.

"I would like to go to Australia," he said. He preferred Australia because my cousin, Jonas Gružauskas, the son of my mother's brother, had gone there and he seemed to like it.

"No! America!" we children cried out in unison. There was no doubt in our minds. We had seen American soldiers and we liked the way they dressed, the way they smoked cigarettes, the way they joked around and laughed. We had seen the power of their guns, their tanks, and their airplanes. They had won the war. They were the conquering heroes.

We also fell in love with America through the movies the soldiers had shown us in the camp on Saturday nights. We saw Betty Grable, the original pinup girl with the million-dollar legs, in one of her many movies. We saw the "Gipper" movie (*Knute Rockne, All American*) with

Ronald Reagan and Pat O'Brien, and we sang along when they played the Notre Dame football song. We sang the American national anthem at the end of the movies as we watched the enormously large stars and stripes fill the background of the entire screen, waving behind the Statue of Liberty, the lady with the long dress proudly raising the torch of freedom. Now we wanted to go to the land that produced those heroes, those movies, those beautiful girls, and those wonderful songs.

We outvoted Dad in number and by the sheer volume of our enthusiasm. Dad understood why we were so enthusiastic about America, but, he pointed out, we'd have to be sponsored by a farmer and he'd be required to work on the farm for two years as an indentured laborer before we'd be allowed to be on our own. He didn't like the idea of what seemed like servitude, something he'd had enough of in his lifetime.

Maybe Dad was right. He had a lot of common sense in those significant situations. That's probably one big reason why we managed to survive and stay together through all those years of turmoil. But we were swept up in the enthusiasm of the moment and didn't want to hear his logical arguments. After six years of the unsettled life in the DP camp, we were anxious to leave behind the grime of post-war Germany and head out to a new life, a new beginning, in the land we had learned to love. Hope had been hung before our eyes and we were prepared to pay any price to follow it.

Later that year, we packed up our few belongings and headed to Bremen, where a D-4-type troopship, the *USS General S. D. Sturgis,* was waiting to carry us across the Atlantic Ocean. It was built by the Kaiser Shipbuilding Corp. in 1943 at Yard No. 3 in Richmond, California, and acquired by the US Navy on March 31, 1944. It was 522 feet in length and was powered by an 8,500-horsepower, geared turbine engine that could propel it to at least sixteen knots. For defense purposes, it was armed with four single 5/38-inch dual-purpose gun mounts, four twin 1.1-inch gun mounts, and fifteen twin 20-mm gun mounts on the deck. Below deck, in multiple tiers, were layers of cots that could sleep almost 5,000 crew and passengers.

We accommodated ourselves several tiers below the deck. It was dark and cramped. The air was heavy from poor circulation and from the smell of diesel oil. It felt like a tomb. We didn't want to remain below deck for very long and only went down there to sleep.

Mom became claustrophobic. She wanted to go to the deck immediately. She took a blanket with her and went up to the deck with my little sister Maria, who was barely two at the time. Diode took Henry with her and followed Mom up to the deck. Weather permitting, they remained up there for most of the trip, which lasted twelve days. Dad attended to the needs of the women and my two younger siblings, Henry and Maria.

The three of us older boys were more active. We were excited about this new adventure and went exploring throughout the entire ship. We examined the guns and the life rafts and all the nooks and crannies of the ship. John had learned some English already and tried to engage the sailors in conversation. They took a shine to him and had him run errands for them.

We cast off in the afternoon of a beautiful, sunny fall day; I think it was October 12, 1950. I felt the powerful engines throbbing below and watched from the aft of the deck the long wake extending toward the receding shoreline. As the large, orange sun sank into the horizon, I remember feeling a sense of awe and momentousness. I knew this was an important event in my life and that I was heading out into an unknown, but hopeful future. I longed to have a real home again, where I would have friends to play with and where there would be no bombing.

It didn't take long, though, for the occasion to deteriorate into something less glamorous. Most of us became seasick, or at least queasy, as soon as we left the harbor and sailed into the rolling waves of the open sea. We stayed that way for the entire twelve days of the crossing. John was an exception. He threw up on the first day and was OK thereafter. He ate all the food that was given to him and occupied himself with helping the sailors. Mom and Maria vomited every day. All Mom could eat was fruit and she kept asking for oranges. My little sister's skin turned yellow. Either she contracted hepatitis or her skin turned yellow from all the oranges she ate.

I did not throw up during the entire trip—a point of pride—though I was always nauseous. I ate very little and, like the others, lost weight. Maria, who was tiny to begin with, became as slender as a reed.

We ran into a storm during the crossing. I watched in fear and amazement as the ship's prow went up into the air, pointing almost directly into the dark sky, and then plowed down into the ocean, shuddering and groaning with the strain until I thought it would never come up again. The waves seemed enormous, especially when the ship's prow went down. They would loom almost directly overhead, like giant leviathans. It seemed impossible that we wouldn't be engulfed by this massive display of nature's raw power. I think I was too frightened to be seasick. I thought about the seesaw we left behind in Lithuania. If the swoop from the ground to the top of the swing was mildly frightening to a five-year-old child, something akin to jumping up and down on a trampoline, this trip in the storm was more like a ride on the largest and most daring roller coaster in the world.

During the height of the storm, the captain stopped the ship and cast anchor. After the storm abated in a day or two, we continued. On the twelfth day, we arrived in New York Harbor. It was the dawn of an overcast Tuesday, the morning of October 24, 1950.

The word flashed through the passengers on the ship: we were approaching the Statue of Liberty. I jumped out of my cot and was up on the deck in an instant. The tugboats chugged us slowly past the lady holding the torch. She was on stage and we were the audience. I had seen her so many times at the end of all those movies. This was the real deal, I kept telling myself; this would be our new home. I'd already forgotten about the storm and the nausea, and I just wished I had a camera.

CHAPTER 8

ELIZABETH, NEW JERSEY

We were processed through Customs and through the Immigration and Naturalization Service right there at the dock after we disembarked from the *USS General S. D. Sturgis.* For some reason, we didn't have to go through Ellis Island, the famous immigrant-processing center we'd heard so much about. Apparently, it was being used as a Coast Guard training base, among other things, at the time. It was finally closed in 1954.

We also found out that we wouldn't have to go to a farm as contract laborers. That was a relief, especially for Dad. Apparently Aunt Eva, who'd arrived in America only six months before, was able to sponsor us, or to "claim" us as relatives, under the second immigration act. Or perhaps enforcement of the act wasn't very strict.

Raudys, our erstwhile neighbor from Plungé, met us at the processing center. He came to pick us up in his car. We were amazed that he had a car.

He'd been in the United States for only a year and had already purchased one. Here was proof positive that America was all that we had dreamed it would be.

"What kind of car is it?" Dad asked Raudys. He was respectful about it, but you could tell he was envious. There had always been a subtle rivalry between Dad and Raudys. Mom would hold Raudys up as an example to Dad whenever she was upset with him for some reason. Raudys didn't drink; he worked hard and was a skilled carpenter. When he came to America with his young wife, Raudys got a job in a factory. After work and on the weekends, he did carpentry work and helped neighbors. Later, after he saved up some money, he bought a parcel of land and built his own home on it. After it was finished, he bought other parcels and built additional houses that he sold for profit. He did what thousands of young immigrants who came to America with nothing but a dream did: he made good through hard work and perseverance.

"It's a Buick," Raudys answered proudly, "a 1948 Buick Roadmaster."

I'm not sure Dad knew that General Motors updated their models every year, but he wanted to show Raudys that he knew something about cars.

"How many cylinders does it have?" Dad asked.

"Eight cylinders; it's a straight eight."

It was a beauty. We clambered into it one by one. There were eight of us: the parents, the five children, and Diode. With Raudys behind the wheel, that made nine. I don't know how we all fit.

Then there were our belongings. We put them in the trunk. Either the trunk was very large or our belongings were few. I think it was the latter.

Raudys drove us into New Jersey via the Holland Tunnel. He pointed out proudly how it was one of the wonders of the world.

"The engineer who built it went insane before it was completed," he added. That sounded somewhat dramatic and made it more awe-inspiring. I found out later, though, that engineer Clifford Milburn Holland, after whom the tunnel was named, died of a heart attack on the operating table while undergoing a tonsillectomy at a health center in Battle Creek, Michigan. That fact was less glamorous than the urban legend of him going insane, although his death was sad enough. He was only forty-one at the time.

Aunt Eva lived in Elizabeth, New Jersey, a city with a population of about 100,000 at the time, located across a narrow tidal strait from Staten Island, not far from New York City. Aunt Eva, Raudys, and we were among about three hundred DP families that settled in Elizabeth in the late 1940s and early 1950s. We were part of what became known as the second wave of perhaps 60,000 Lithuanian immigrants who left their homeland near the end of World War II. There was already a sizeable Lithuanian community when we got there, numbering about five thousand. Many were already second- or third-generation Lithuanian-Americans.

The original Lithuanian immigrants, the first wave, started to settle there in 1878 due, in part, to the employment available at the Singer sewing machine plant built in 1872. After settling in, they organized themselves and formed a fraternal organization, the Saint Kazimir Beneficial Society, in December 1891. In 1895, they built a church, Saints Peter and Paul Lithuanian Roman Catholic Church, at 216 Ripley Place. It added a spiritual dimension to the social fabric and identity of the Lithuanian immigrants. In October 1913, a group formed the Lithuanian Building and Loan Association, which, in turn, financed the building in 1924 of Lithuanian Liberty Hall, a community center with a hall for social affairs, meeting rooms, a sizeable bar, and four bowling lanes. I set pins there for several years after I turned sixteen.

Aunt Eva lived in a one-bedroom apartment with her daughter and her mom, my grandmother. It was located on the second floor of a small house on Pine Street, in the port area near Newark Bay and the Kill Van Kull tidal strait. The first floor had been converted to a retail store. The front wall had been replaced with a large display window, but when the neighborhood deteriorated, the store closed. When we got there, the large display window had already been boarded up. Inside were some counters, small pieces of furniture and miscellaneous boxes, all covered with a thick layer of dust. No one had been inside for years.

Dad and we three older boys spent our first night there, as well as the next several weeks, until we were able to rent an apartment of our own. Mom, Henry, Maria, and Diode slept upstairs, on the floor.

There was no heat in the boarded-up store. The weather had turned colder and a severe rainstorm with strong winds hit the area. It lasted for several days. I came down with a bad cold and an ear infection.

The next morning, Ray and I ventured out into the backyard to look around. We wanted to get our first taste of this new land. The trip over the Atlantic Ocean, the Statue of Liberty, and the grand scale of everything that had happened to us in the last several months were still swirling about in my brain. I was hoping to experience some sort of a significant event, something to tell me that we were here, at last, and that this was to be our home from now on; a welcome maybe, or some sort of a sign, at least.

It didn't happen. We did run into several boys, though. They were the children of the landlord. They were a little older than we, well into their teen years. They seemed friendly and made an effort to engage us in a conversation. Once they realized that we had no idea of what they were talking about, they resorted to gestures and pictures. They brought out a couple of

Police Gazette-type magazines with pictures of women posing in negligees, revealing dresses, or some sort of underwear.

"Do you like the pictures?" the older one asked us, with a knowing smile.

I smiled back timidly, but wasn't sure of what to say. I liked girls, all right, but I wasn't used to explicit displays of sex. Sex was never discussed in our house, and we boys who discussed it amongst ourselves treated the subject with a kind of mysterious wonderment and mythology.

I also learned, after we arrived in Elizabeth, that the term "DP" had another meaning. As used by some of the kids in the neighborhood, it was a putdown, much like "wop," "kike," or "Pollack." When Dennis, a boy who lived across the street from us, lost some of his marbles to me in a game of Ringer, he stood up abruptly and left, sneering, "Dumb DP," over his shoulder.

In retrospect, it was reassuring to know that we weren't being singled out; we were treated just as badly as all the other immigrant groups. I ran into Dennis several times after that and got even with him by besting him in a street scuffle. But as I got older, I began to realize that the putdown version of the term wasn't far off the mark. We were poor, uneducated, and at the bottom of the social strata, even in a blue-collar town like Elizabeth, New Jersey. It didn't take long for me to figure out that the America I had learned to love by watching Betty Grable, Clark Gable, and Ronald Regan movies at the DP camp in Germany would be a lot tougher to become part of than the Hollywood dream machine made it look.

The first challenge was money. Mom and Dad got jobs right after we arrived, but they didn't earn much. Mom found work at Hollander

& Sons, an umbrella factory where Aunt Eva was employed. We arrived in New York on Tuesday, October 24, 1950, and Mom followed Aunt Eva to the factory on Wednesday, October 25. She worked there as a sewing machine operator until the factory closed twenty years later. I don't think she missed a day of work in those twenty years, even when she was sick.

Dad worked at a number of different places at first, mostly factories, including the Singer sewing machine plant. Eventually he got a job he stuck with at the General Motors assembly plant in Linden, New Jersey. Much like the other jobs he'd had, the work at GM was repetitive and boring, but the pay and benefits were better there than the other places. For a man with little education and broken English, it was the best he could hope for. He worked there until age sixty-five, when he retired with a company pension and Social Security benefits.

We lived from paycheck to paycheck. After food, clothing, and shelter, there wasn't much left over to spread around to us kids. And when Dad blew his paycheck on one of his periodic weekend binges, things got a little tighter.

I decided to see if I could make a few dollars. I was only twelve at the time and couldn't get a real job, but I could shine shoes, I decided.

"Mom," I said one Saturday morning, "I want to go to the farmers' market with you today."

"Sure," she said. "No problem. I could always use the help."

"Yeah, I want to help you," I said.

"You're not usually so cooperative." She looked at me suspiciously. "What's going on?"

"Oh, nothing," I responded, trying to muster a tone of sincerity. "I mean, I'm growing up already and I have to take on more responsibilities."

"Well, I'm glad to hear that. You sound more mature," she said in a tone of encouragement.

"I mean I'm getting old enough where I could earn some money."

"How do you plan to do that?"

"I want to shine shoes, just like Ray."

"Well, you're a little young yet, but I guess it would be OK. We could always use a little extra money."

"Great! I'll build a shoeshine box out of the vegetable boxes they throw out at the farmers' market."

"Sounds like a plan."

"Oh, there's just one other thing: I need to buy a metal foot rest, some shoe polish, and brushes."

"Now I see what all this mature cooperation is about; you need some money."

"Yes, but I'll pay you back. Honest."

"OK, but you'll have to turn over the earnings to me. I'll keep them safe for you."

I built a shoeshine box out of the soft pine boards from a vegetable box I picked up at the farmers' market. Mom staked me a few dollars to buy a metal footrest, black and brown shoe polish, and two brushes. Then I went off to the bars, looking for customers.

My usual stops were at the taverns on lower Second Street: Club 315, Lithuanian Liberty Hall, and Big Paul's Saloon. Club 315 wasn't too good; it had few customers, mostly surly, and not much of an atmosphere. I rarely got a hit there. Lithuanian Liberty Hall was better, but not by much. Most of the customers were Lithuanian DPs, like us. They weren't much into appearances. They worked in construction or factory jobs and just came in to tie one on with their friends after work. They didn't care much about having their dirty and/or muddy safety shoes shined. Once in a while, I came across retired types who wore Florsheim wing tips and got to shine them.

Big Paul's was usually the best. It was a small bar for serious drinkers and was the liveliest, especially on weekends. It didn't take many customers to make it feel pleasantly crowded. Big Paul's ample girth and his friendly but no-nonsense personality attracted men from the neighborhood along with a few of their wives or girlfriends. On weekends, or on cold winter nights, especially when it rained or snowed, Big Paul's was standing-room only. The shot-and-beer crowd filled the place with cigarette smoke, jukebox music, and loud conversations. If the noise level lulled temporarily, there was always the bright TV set sitting on a platform above the bar. Some programs, such as the Bob Hope specials for the troops that featured gorgeous Hollywood starlets, would draw the crowd's attention. *Your Show of Shows* with Sid Caesar, Imogene Coca, Carl Reiner, and Howard Morris was another favorite. *The Ed Sullivan Show* was a must on Sunday nights.

I usually found customers there who liked getting a shoeshine—and most of them were good tippers. Even though the going rate was ten or fifteen cents a shine, I often got a quarter or more.

I did have a couple of problems early on, though. One was that I didn't have the "right stuff" for shining shoes. I knew the mechanics of it; it wasn't that complicated. You put the wax on, let it dry a bit, and then buffed it off with a rag. But there was more to it; a style, you might say. First, you put the polish on with your fingers, not a cloth or a brush, and you did it quickly. Then you buffed the shoe with the rag, except that you did it smartly, making the rag snap from time to time. You had to put on a bit of a show.

I watched the other boys shine shoes and tried to imitate them. It took me a while to get the hang of it. The first few times, I ended up smearing polish on customers' socks. That wasn't too cool. Some of the nicer men teased me about it, though. They asked if I charged extra for shining their socks.

Which brings me to the other problem I had: English. If a man tried to engage me in a conversation, humorous or otherwise, I was in trouble. I'd look blankly at him until I got some idea of what he was saying. If he looked back at me with a twinkle in his beer-glazed eyes, I'd smile and nod affirmatively. If not, I'd mumble something about "no speaka da Inglis" and slink away. Most of the men asked me where I was from before they let me go.

Everybody in the neighborhood seemed to like Big Paul's, even the kids. I learned from Vyto, one of my DP friends, that there was a song about Big Paul's, an anthem of sorts. It was sung to the tune of the "Caisson Song," or the "Army Song," as it later came to be known. It went something like this:

> *Give a cheer, give a cheer, to the men that drink the beer*
> *In the backroom of Big Paul's saloon.*
>
> *They are brave, they are bold, for the whiskey that they hold*
> *In the backroom of Big Paul's saloon.*

Whenever I heard the tune played in a military parade or a movie, I'd sing along, using the words from Big Paul's saloon.

When I got home from making the rounds at the neighborhood bars, Mom would ask how much I made. That was the clue that she wanted me to give her the money. She used it to supplement the family budget, she said. Once in a while, she'd let me have a quarter or fifty cents for spending, but not often. She didn't want me to spend it on frivolous things, like soda or candy or comic books. Some of my friends told me I was crazy to give her all the money, but whenever I protested, Mom persuaded me that I was doing it for the good of the family. When I got tired of hearing that argument, she'd use the alternate one: she was saving the money on my behalf for my future. I never saw that nest egg. But in all fairness to Mom, I had a roof over my head and food on the table.

On Saturdays, in the fall and winter months, I worked for a man named Carl. I never knew his last name. Carl was a small, Jewish entrepreneur with a penchant for making a buck. He might have been in his early forties at the time, though his grizzly beard and gravelly voice made him seem older. Carl would pick me up, along with the other kids who worked for him, in his rickety panel truck early in the morning, usually about 6:30. He'd drive each of us to our locations and leave us there with a basket of fresh pretzels. He usually took me to the intersection of Trumbull and Division Streets, where I'd stay until the middle of the afternoon. I got a commission for each pretzel I sold, something like five cents a pretzel. Some days I'd sell a lot of them, especially if it was cold; other days I'd climb back into Carl's panel truck with the basket still full of pretzels.

When I got home from selling pretzels, I'd give all the money to Mom. Sometimes I'd go right back out that same evening to shine shoes. I also branched out into other enterprises. For a time, I collected newspapers and sold them to a recycling center, although that venture didn't last long. Paper was cheap and you had to come up with hundreds of pounds of it to make even a few dollars. I did better with empty soda bottles. I'd get a few cents for each one when I took them to a store. If I brought back three or four empties, I could buy a full bottle with the refunds. That barter deal was a double win: I got the instant gratification of a sugary soda while avoiding having to report the money to Mom.

During the summer months, I'd either go to the shore of the Arthur Kill strait or, better yet, to the city garbage dump where you could find returnable bottles and other kinds of neat stuff, like metal objects. Metals, like copper, would fetch a decent price at some junkyards, I learned.

CHAPTER 9
THE NEW AND THE OLD

They placed me, along with my brother Ray and our cousin Irene, in the fifth grade at Saints Peter and Paul Catholic Grammar School. (Many elementary schools were called "grammar schools" in those days.) I was eleven, about the same age as the other kids, but Ray and Irene were older. Ray was fifteen already and should've been in high school; Irene was twelve and should have been in seventh or eighth grade. As best as I can surmise, though, we were all placed in the fifth grade because Sister Christine, a nun from the Order of Saint Francis, was the fifth-grade teacher and spoke some Lithuanian. Since none of us spoke any English yet, I guess the thinking was that she would translate for us.

It didn't work out that way. For the first two days, Sister Christine stopped the lessons every so often and explained things to us in Lithuanian, but it was too disruptive for the rest of the class. So she assigned "buddies" to us who were supposed to help us. My buddy was

Vyto Maceikonis, the one who taught me Big Paul's "anthem." He'd arrived the year before and was already somewhat conversant in English. He translated for me a few times, but it didn't take long for him to become annoyed by my questions. Whenever I'd look at him for an explanation after that, he'd let me know, with a grunt, that I was on my own.

I don't remember the details of what happened to Ray and Irene, but I don't think they fared much better. Ray dropped out of school as soon as he turned sixteen; Irene finished the eighth grade before she quit.

Even after my English improved, I had trouble with some of the subjects, such as diagramming a sentence. That was the grammar exercise in which a sentence was broken down into a series of lines, each line representing a part of the sentence, such as the subject, object, verb, adjective, adverb, preposition, modifier, etc. Those lines drove me nuts. I had no idea what Sister Christine was talking about. As hard as I tried, I couldn't make sense of it. If she called on me to place a word on one of the lines, I'd guess wildly. Once in a while, I guessed right, but more often than not, the look of exasperation on her face told me I didn't get it.

Besides the language, there were cultural differences that took a while to get used to—like what they showed on TV, for example. The whole concept of whooping it up with scantily dressed dancing girls and comedians trying to make you laugh seemed odd to me. Lithuanian public entertainment was more structured, controlled, and officially approved. At least that's what I remembered. We'd go to plays, operas, concerts, and so on, but they didn't feature scantily clad women, comedians, or the whooping and dancing that we saw on TV.

That's not to say that we didn't let our hair down once in a while, or loosen our collars, so to speak. We did that plenty, but it was something we did privately with friends. After we bought our first television set, however, it didn't take long for me to start enjoying programs like *The Ed Sullivan Show*, *The Hit Parade*, and *I Love Lucy*.

One thing I had no trouble getting used to was cartoons. In Germany, I had seen American comic books, such as *Superman, Katzenjammer Kids,* and *Donald Duck*. Any money I was able to get hold of in Elizabeth, I spent on comic books. They cost ten cents each, except for the "classic series," which were a quarter. I wasn't interested in the classic series at first, but as I got older, I began to collect the more literary material, like *Mutiny on the Bounty, Robinson Crusoe,* and *Captain Courageous*.

Animated cartoons were the best. The movies we went to see were usually preceded by animated cartoons, such as the Looney Tunes and Merrie Melodies films by Warner Bros. starring Bugs Bunny, Daffy Duck, or Porky Pig. I loved them. For me, that was the main reason to go to the movies. The fast-paced Woody Woodpecker song with the Mel Blanc laugh that started and ended the cartoons transported me to a joyous state of pure fun. The main feature was almost a sidelight, though I stayed on to get my quarter's worth.

Marbles were another thing I took to without any trouble. I learned that you could accumulate lots of them by beating other kids at the game of Ringer. I became a decent shooter and started to beat some of the kids on our block. I played with Dennis regularly and usually took him for all the marbles he had, mostly because he was hotheaded and would blow his cool easily. After a while, though, I lost interest in marbles. You couldn't do much with them after you collected them. Henry and Maria would scatter them all over the house. That made the parents angry and they'd make me pick them up. So I gave up marbles in favor of comic books, looking for empty soda bottles, or just hanging out with the guys.

Like me, the guys I usually hung out with were all recent Lithuanian immigrants. They lived in the neighborhood and attended Saints Peter and Paul Catholic Grammar School. One of them was Vyto, my erstwhile English-language coach. Vyto (he liked to be called "Mack") was bigger than I was, and almost a year older. Because of his size and self-confidence, he was one of the leaders of the group. He had a strong ego and wanted his point of view to prevail regardless of whether we were offering opinions on some topic, discussing facts, or deciding what we were going to do next. It usually did, except when Vyto Didžbalis took a different position. Vyto D. was a rival to Mack for the position of alpha male. The two Vytos didn't always get along.

Vyto D. wasn't as tall as Mack, but he was every bit as strong—probably stronger. He had two older brothers who were even stronger, so he had to be tough to survive. Also, he was more of a street fighter than Mack was. His father was a steady drinker, probably an alcoholic like my dad and the fathers of most of my friends.

Then there was Ray Bakšys. Ray was a small, skinny kid like me. He became one of my best friends, mainly because he was one of the few kids who didn't make fun of me. He was easy to get along with and wasn't territorial, like the two Vytos were. He didn't have to be. He was a good-looking boy with blond hair and became very popular with girls. He drifted away from our group as he got older and teamed up with the American gang from Johnny's restaurant, which included girls. They were into hanging around the restaurant and listening to rock-and-roll music, which was just beginning to emerge. That and drinking, of course.

Finally, there was Joe Stagniunas. Joe, a mild-mannered boy, was among the more thoughtful members of the group. While he wasn't any fonder of school than the rest of us, he liked to read. He wasn't a sissy, though. He could take care of himself and I sort of adopted him as my buddy after Ray drifted away. I sought him out whenever I could, but he was more of a friend to Mack, his cousin, than he was to me.

Despite our similar backgrounds, however, I never felt particularly close to those boys. I longed to recapture the feeling of closeness I'd felt with the kids in the DP camp in Germany. I also thought about Rasa and wondered what had happened to her. I wondered what city she'd moved to in America and whether she still remembered me.

One day, when I was about fifteen, I saw her brother's picture in *Darbininkas,* a Lithuanian newspaper published in New York. His name was Saulius. He was named in the caption under the picture and in a brief article about a summer Scout camp in Massachusetts. Apparently, Saulius and other Lithuanian Boy Scouts and Girl Scouts were going to attend that camp.

I was thrilled to discover a lead to my first and only love. I mobilized the best detective skills I could muster to track her down. It didn't take a brain surgeon to figure out that she probably lived with her brother. I called the newspaper and asked for Saulius's address.

"I'm sorry," the person at the newspaper said. "We don't give out such information."

"Please," I pleaded. "Saulius was a good friend of mine in Germany. I've been trying to track him down for some years."

I left out the part that I was really after his sister.

"This is very irregular," the man said, seeming to waver. "Let me speak to the reporter who wrote the story."

"Thank you. Thank you," I gushed. "Your help would be greatly appreciated."

The newsman was reluctant at first, but my enthusiasm and sincerity must've swayed him. After checking with the reporter, he called me back with the address.

As luck would have it, Rasa and her brother lived in Brooklyn, only thirty or forty miles from Elizabeth. I wrote a letter to Rasa asking whether she planned to attend the Scout camp. Even though I hadn't joined the Boy Scouts yet, I told a little white lie: I said I was hoping to go to that camp with my troop in New Jersey.

She wrote back saying that she and her brother did indeed plan to go to the Scout camp with their troops and, furthermore, the New York and New Jersey troops were scheduled to go to Massachusetts on the same bus.

I was overwhelmed with joy. Hearing from her renewed all the feelings I'd had for her in Germany. I couldn't sleep in anticipation of seeing that tiny, bashful girl again. I immediately joined the Boy Scout troop in New Jersey and signed up for the trip to the camp in Massachusetts. I talked Mom into putting up the money for the trip. Father wasn't too enthusiastic about the expense, so I had to promise to pay them back.

On the day of the trip, we boarded the bus in front of the Lithuanian Liberty Hall and headed to New York to pick up the Brooklyn troop. When we arrived, I stuck my head out the window, looking for Rasa. Before I could spot her, though, another girl walked up to me on the bus and introduced herself.

"Hi," she said with a nice smile, "my name is Birute."

"Hi," I said. She was pretty enough, but I was expecting Rasa.

"I'm a friend of Rasa," she went on. "She told me you'd be on the bus."

I didn't know what to say and craned my neck to see if I could spot Rasa. "We lived in Kempten also, in the same DP camp," she went on. "You and I were in the same class."

I didn't remember her, probably because I only had eyes for Rasa at the time. I glanced briefly at her. She was petite and pretty, with beautiful blond hair, and very friendly. She sat down next to me and began to tell me what she remembered about Germany. As I listened to her, I kept looking for Rasa.

Finally, Rasa boarded the bus and said "hi" to me as she passed by. My heart stopped when I looked at her. Feelings of confusion began to overtake me. Rasa appeared to be a good foot taller than I was and not at all bashful. She didn't show any interest in me and only gave me a perfunctory greeting. She had learned to be teenage cool, I guess, and apparently, I wasn't cool enough. I felt crushed.

I turned to the girl sitting next to me. Birute kept up a lively chatter; she seemed to like me. That was some consolation.

The author; circa 1956

CHAPTER 10
TEEN YEARS

My teen years were filled with as much confusion, doubt, and angst as any other teenager's, except that mine had an immigrant's twist to them. After graduating from Saints Peter and Paul in 1953, I was enrolled in a public school, the Grover Cleveland Junior High School. That was a completely new experience. If I felt like an outsider at Saints Peter and Paul, it was nothing compared to Grover Cleveland. There were hundreds of kids enrolled in the school and I didn't know any of them. Some of the kids from my grammar school were enrolled there, but none was in my homeroom. I felt lost.

Then there was the question of the pecking order. While I was never completely happy with my place among the boys at Saints Peter and Paul, I did have a niche of sorts. At Grover Cleveland, I was a nonentity. Most of the kids simply ignored me, although some of the more aggressive ones got on my case just to make life miserable for me. Not having an identity, or a group to shield me, I was fair game for the bullies.

I tried to avoid the mean ones and learned how to "dance," as I called it, with the others. Dancing meant asking a lot of questions, laughing a lot, and acting like a clown sometimes. I didn't relish that role, but I didn't have much choice: either I danced or everyone simply ignored me. No one made an effort to befriend me.

Size was another problem. While a few boys at grammar school were bigger and stronger than I was, they were midgets compared with some of the boys at Grover Cleveland. There was this one Polish guy—"Stash" was his name—who'd grab me from behind, wrap his arms around my chest, lift me off the ground by leaning back, and squeeze me until I either fainted from a lack of oxygen or cried uncle.

I usually cried uncle. I was used to being at least a medium-sized fish in a small pond; here I was one of the plankton for the whales.

Then there were the black kids. I'd never been around them before. There were no blacks in Lithuania and very few in Germany, except for the mulatto souvenirs of black American GIs and blonde German girls. In our eyes, blacks were strange creatures and we didn't know what to make of them. After we came to the United States, we didn't have much to do with them. We stayed in our neighborhood, which was ethnic European, and the blacks stayed in theirs. Sure, I'd see them from a distance, but I never had to interact with them. None attended our church and none was enrolled at the grammar school. I'd hear their music occasionally on the higher end of the radio dial, but that was about it.

I was fascinated by the sound of that music, though. It was very different from the popular music of the day. If Dad heard me listening to it, he'd make some disparaging remarks about it being "wild" music and make me turn it off. A few "safe" blacks, like Louis Armstrong, Nat King

Cole, and later, Johnny Mathis, crossed over into the popular culture, but they remained an exception to the general rule.

Blacks weren't acknowledged in those days—at least not publicly. They were there, but they weren't. Unofficially, the feeling among the whites was that blacks were to be tolerated, as long as they "knew their place." At least that seemed to be the general feeling of the middle class. Down at the lower end of the social scale, where we were, the distinction wasn't that clear. We weren't any more enlightened about race relations than the middle class was, but we lived closer to blacks and ran into them more often, especially if we attended public schools. After I enrolled at Grover Cleveland, they were there suddenly, in my classes, in the gym, in the hallways, everywhere. They looked funny; they smelled funny. Some of them would put something in their hair to straighten out its natural kinkiness. I guess they were emulating some of the popular black entertainers of that era, such as Chuck Berry, Little Richard, and James Brown. The smell was terrible, though. I found out later that it was called "conk" (short for "congolene"), a gel made from lye. Some kids made conk at home by mixing lye, eggs, and potatoes, which accounts for the very unpleasant aroma.

I was very uneasy about it and didn't know how to react to it. I knew enough not to say anything about the smell, though. That would be impolite. Besides, they might turn on me and beat me up.

After a while, I learned few things about interacting with black kids. I was told to stay away from them, especially if they were athletes; if I crossed them up, they'd gang up on me and beat me up—maybe even kill me. Some were rumored to carry weapons. Even Stash kept his distance from them. We could talk about them among ourselves, maybe even make fun of them, but we didn't dare do it openly.

This was way out of my league. All I could do was kind of look sideways at them in the boys' shower. I guess they'd learned how to take care of themselves. They had established—among the boys, at least—a pecking order; it was near the top. And while they were never part of the white groups at Grover Cleveland Junior High, they were treated as equals in power, which was more than was the case in society at large.

The Civil Rights movement was just gearing up around that time. On May 17, 1954, the United States Supreme Court handed down a unanimous decision on *Brown v. Board of Education of Topeka* holding that the establishment of separate public schools for black and white students was inherently unequal. It overturned its1896 decision in *Plessy v. Ferguson,* which had upheld a state law requiring "separate but equal" segregated facilities for blacks and whites in railway cars.

On August 28, 1955, Emmett Till, a fourteen-year-old black boy from Chicago was brutally murdered in the Mississippi Delta region by several white men who thought that Till had made a pass at the wife of one of them. After Till's body was recovered from the Tallahatchie River, his mother had the body shipped back to Chicago where she displayed it in an open casket. The body may have been embalmed but no reconstruction was done to enhance his appearance. The black community was outraged, especially after the two men accused of killing Till were acquitted at trial. (Years later, they admitted to committing the crime.)

On December 1, 1955, Rosa Parks, a seamstress in Montgomery, Alabama, was arrested and charged with violating racial segregation ordinances in Montgomery by refusing to give up her seat on a bus to a white man. She was found guilty and fined ten dollars plus court costs of four dollars. The black citizens of Montgomery organized around several black church leaders, including the Reverend Martin Luther King

Jr., and started a bus boycott. The whites fought back with cross burnings by the Ku Klux Klan, as well as fire bombings of four black Baptist churches and the homes of Martin Luther King and Ralph Abernathy. But the boycott continued until the US Supreme Court struck down Montgomery's bus segregation ordinances.

The impact of those events and court decisions was indirect on us in Elizabeth. I sensed the winds of change beginning to blow, but change came slowly. There was a lot of controversy and anger among whites who felt that the blacks were making too many unreasonable demands. Many of the poor whites I knew felt that they had to struggle very hard to build a better life for themselves and for their families, and that the blacks were trying to take a shortcut to success.

I tried to stay away from the controversy; I had too many problems of my own. For one thing, I never felt that I fit in with the white boys, much less with the blacks. Many of the white boys my age, especially the Italian ones, had "DA" (duck's ass) haircuts and wore pegged pants and pointed shoes. Pegged pants required tapering at the bottom; the pants had to be long enough so that there would be a break in the crease.

I didn't understand why pants had to be pegged, and didn't really like them that way, but I decided to try it. I wanted to blend in. The next time Mom bought a pair of slacks for me, I had the tailor taper them. The tailor, a kindly old Jewish man with a small shop on Third Street, wasn't quite sure of what I wanted. Neither was I. So he cut them as best as he could, based on the way I explained the style to him.

I probably didn't explain it very well. The first day I wore them to school was a disaster. During recess, when all the students were in the yard, a boy with a mane of blond hair combed back into a DA noticed the pants and started making fun of them. "Holy shit!" he shouted, pointing to my pants, "look at this guy."

In a matter of seconds, it seemed like the entire school had gathered around me and was laughing at my pants. I felt like crawling under the chain-link fence. I was too paralyzed with shame and embarrassment to move. Finally, Mack, who was beside me, whispered urgently, "Get the heck out of here."

I followed that advice. And I never wore those pants again. Mom was upset with me because she had spent all that money to buy and alter them. In spite of her repeated efforts, I wouldn't give in. There was no way I was going to go through that humiliation again. She then tried to persuade Ray, who was about my size, to wear them, but he wanted no part of them either. She had to accept the fact that those pants were a social pariah and a financial loss.

During the summer months, we went swimming in the public pool. Dozens of kids, maybe a hundred or more, including some black kids, filled the pool with their bodies, their noise, their splashing, their jumping, and their shouting. I loved to go there whenever I could. The entrance fee was only a quarter and I could come up with it by turning in a few empty pop bottles.

There were also girls there—in bathing suits. That was another attraction. One of the guys I knew from school told me he liked to bump into girls to get a quick feel. One girl in particular, he said, liked it when the guys were rough with her and enjoyed being felt up. He encouraged me to try it.

I had seen the girl he was talking about but I wasn't really friendly with her. I saw her at the pool one Saturday afternoon in the shallow area and waded over to her. She seemed to be by herself, although she was in the midst of the crowd of cavorting kids. Getting into the festive spirit of the occasion, I kind of bumped into her, dunked her under water, and generally engaged her in horseplay. She responded to my interest, but it didn't get very far. I wasn't very good at pretending to do one thing when I was really trying to do something else. It seemed dishonest. The "loose" girl messed around with me for a while, but soon lost interest in my bumbling efforts.

Some of my DP friends liked to climb up to the high diving board and jump into the pool, if not in a graceful swan dive, at least feet first. They would fold their legs under their butts and hold them in place with their hands with the goal of seeing who could make the biggest splash. They urged me to jump from the diving board, but I usually declined. They called me a chicken, thinking that I was afraid of the height. I wasn't. It was because my right eardrum was perforated from scarlet fever I'd had as a child in Germany, and the few times I jumped from the diving board, I came down with a raging ear infection.

After spending the afternoon in the pool, we'd go to the locker room to shower and change into street clothes. The rowdy mood from the pool would continue in the locker room, where the boys horsed around, snapping wet towels at bare butts, and making fun of each other. The neat thing in the locker room was the speaker system. It was hooked up to a radio station that played the popular tunes of the day. I remember hearing, for the first time, Tony Bennett singing "Because of You" in his lyrical tenor and Johnnie Ray singing "Cry" in his inimitable style. The boys would stop horsing around when those songs came on and sing along lustily.

I was fascinated by music's magic power to transform these rough boys into friendly, laughing kids. I didn't identify yet with the music they seemed to like. I was more attuned to the mainstream music that radio stations at the center of the dial were still playing—the standards composed by Tin Pan Alley-era giants like Irving Berlin, Jerome Kern, and Cole Porter and recorded by singers such as Frank Sinatra, Doris Day, Rosemary Clooney, the Andrew Sisters, and Patti Page. Tony Bennett and Johnnie Ray were a shift from that. It was the beginning of the rock-and-roll era and I wasn't sure how to react to it. Although it didn't take long to like Tony Bennett, Johnnie Ray was more of a stretch. He had a strange, raspy voice and sang around a tune; he didn't let the tune dictate his style and interpretation of the music. One of his biggest hits was the song "Cry." When he sang it on TV, he'd writhe on the floor in seeming agony, or beat up his piano in anger. This was something new and kids responded to his emotion and antiauthoritarian histrionics.

Even more radical was the music played by stations at the high end of the dial. I thought it was only for black listeners and never paid much attention to it. Then I walked into Johnny's Restaurant one day and heard white boys and girls my age singing along with the music—and they weren't even listening to the radio; they were feeding nickels into the jukebox that was stacked with 45-rpm vinyl records.

That sound was weird: a lot of harmonies, usually sung by black men or women, and refrains made up nonsensical sounds like "shoobee doowap," backed by heavy rhythm. The Five Satins recorded "In the Still of the Night"; the del Vikings sang "Come Go with Me"; the Coasters had big hits with "Yakety Yak" and "Charley Brown"; Little Anthony and The Imperials grooved "Tears on my Pillow"; the Rays had boys and girls crooning "Silhouettes"; and the Penguins scored with "Earth Angel." I couldn't believe how passionate these kids from Second Street were about the music.

Don't get me wrong; I liked music. I liked it a lot. For a kid who didn't have too many diversions in his life (no summer camp, no bike, no trips to visit relatives, no nothing), radio music was one of the few things I could enjoy for free. But I liked to tune in WNEW on Saturday mornings and listen to *The Make Believe Ballroom* where the deejay, William B. Williams, played tunes like Hoagy Carmichael's "Stardust Melody" and a lot of stuff by Frank Sinatra, whom he called "the Chairman of the Board."

Country and western music was another new sound to me, although it didn't sound as strange as rhythm and blues and what came to be known as rock and roll. My brother Ray liked country and western music. He was working already and could afford to buy 45-rpm vinyl records. I told him that many people considered it lowbrow music, but I couldn't dissuade him from listening to it.

"Why do you like that music?" I asked him one day as he sang along to a 45-rpm vinyl record on the RCA Victrola phonograph. "It's hillbilly music."

"What do you care," he retorted. "You're too stupid, anyway."

After a while I started to like country music, too, especially songs by artists like Hank Williams, who managed to cross over into the mainstream with "Your Cheatin' Heart," "Hey, Good Looking," and "I Can't Help It If I'm Still in Love with You"; Patsy Cline, who scored big with "Walkin' After Midnight," and "I Fall to Pieces"; and the classic, "Crazy," written by Willie Nelson.

While the summer afternoons in the pool were fun, they often ended up with a trip to the doctor. I had a perforated ear drum in my right ear from early childhood and didn't realize that I should wear an ear plug when I went swimming. So it would become infected and I had to spend time in the waiting room of a second-or third-generation Lithuanian doc-tor, who would prescribe penicillin for me even though my parents usually didn't have money to pay him. He'd let me clean up around his office or run errands for him in lieu of payment. Sometimes he'd have me straighten up the waiting room after the patients had gone; other times I took the gar-bage out or ran to the store to buy cigarettes or soda pop for him.

Sometimes he'd forget I was there. I'd sit in the waiting room for an hour or more, waiting for him to tell me what he wanted me to do. After all the patients left, I'd read his magazines, especially *Esquire,* which often had pictures of pretty girls wearing lots of makeup and scanty clothing, as well as drawings of the famous Vargas pin-up girls.

Since his office was in his home, he'd go upstairs to the living quar-ters and have a drink after he was done with his patients. He drank quite a bit. His wife would often get on his case about the drinking and loud arguments would break out. I'd half-listen to the argument while flipping through the pages of *Esquire.* As long as I heard him arguing, I could look at *Esquire* without being discovered, although I kept the good ear alert for the muffled sounds of shoes on carpeting approaching the waiting room, just to be on the safe side.

One time I must've gotten too engrossed in the magazine and he walked in without my hearing him. He noticed my look of guilt and gave me a half-hearted lecture on the birds and bees. He died shortly thereafter, following a heart attack. I don't think my parents ever paid him what they owed him; I don't think he kept track.

I also had some dental problems at the time—the usual stuff, like cavi-ties. Mom and Dad didn't have enough money to send us for regular care, so when things got bad enough we'd go to a dentist who accepted pay-ment through a government assistance program. This dentist emphasized quantity over quality. He pulled out several of my teeth when I was about twelve. Either he thought they were too decayed, or he decided it would be less time-consuming to extract them than to fix them. In any case, he told me I was young enough that they'd be replaced with adult teeth.

They weren't—at least not completely. They came out about halfway and then stopped. That gave my dentures an uneven appearance, which was accentuated by a broken front tooth, thanks to Ray. He and I were horsing around one day with an army canteen we'd brought over from Germany. We both wanted it for some silly reason. I grabbed it from him and held it out laughingly in front of him as if to say, "There, I beat you." At that moment, he kicked the canteen. It flipped over the handle that I was holding and broke my front tooth in half.

Mom and Dad couldn't afford to put a cap on it, so it remained that way throughout high school. After I graduated and got a job, I had it capped. I must've been about nineteen or twenty at the time. I also had caps fitted on the two teeth that never fully grew in. For the first time in many years, I could smile naturally, although it still took a while before I lost my self-consciousness about it.

Other than the dental problems and the ear infections, I was pretty healthy, strong, and athletic. My reflexes and my balance were excellent. I could've been good in some sports, though I never tried out for any. I don't know why; maybe it was because no one asked. None of my DP friends played sports and my parents never encouraged me.

One time, though, the high school gym teacher tested the entire class for strength, balance, and flexibility. He made us do push-ups, sit-ups, cartwheels, and things like raising ourselves on our hands from a sitting position. Out of a class of more than a hundred, I was one of the few students to pass all of the tests. The teacher pulled us aside. "We're going to have a trampoline show in a few months. I want to train you guys to perform. We'll have to have practice every day after school."

As I listened to him, I was thrilled at the prospect of performing in the show. This was a chance to prove myself; to get some respect from the other kids.

"You're going to perform in a special assembly of all the students and their families," he went on, "including yours."

I nodded with enthusiasm.

"Now here are two permission slips," he said, handing us several pieces of paper. "One is for you parents to sign; the other one is for your doctor."

That seemed easy enough. All I had to do was get permission from my parents and the family doctor to participate.

The parents said OK. They signed the permission slip, probably without really knowing what they were signing. The good doctor who treated me without charge, on the other hand, refused. He thought it might be a problem because of my ear infections.

I was crushed. I wanted so badly to perform in front of the whole school. When the performance was put on some months later, I would've done anything to be on that stage. It would've been the first time in my life that someone had believed enough in me to give me a chance to prove myself.

CHAPTER 11
KELLY'S POOLROOM

It was a Saturday morning in the spring of 1956. Rocky Marciano had just retired as the undefeated heavyweight boxing champion of the world and the radio stations were playing Doris Day's recording of "Que Será, Será." I ran out of our rented apartment looking for something to do. I didn't want to be home; Mom and Dad argued a lot, usually about money, although with so many other problems, they never had a shortage of topics. When they got tired of arguing with each other, they'd get on our cases to pick up our clothes, help out around the house, or do our homework.

When Dad came home from work, he was tired. The job he had on the assembly line at the General Motors plant in Linden was tough. Some nights, especially on paydays, he didn't come home at all; he went drinking. Mom would go out to look for him before he spent all the money that she had earmarked for food and rent. At first, he'd go to local neighborhood bars and Mom would find him without too much trouble.

After a while, though, he started to expand his range to black neighborhoods where Mom was afraid to go—although she did anyway.

I didn't know which was worse, Mom and Dad arguing, them getting on our cases, or Mom running around frantically looking for Dad in the black bars. So I tried to get away from the house every chance I got. That usually meant going out into the street to look for some of the guys. On this Saturday, I walked over to Second Street, by Johnny's Restaurant, and ran into Rossi. I knew Rossi from the high school, although he'd just dropped out. He was nice-looking, quiet, respectful, and polite. He had a small group of friends on Second Street, including the regulars at Johnny's Restaurant. They hung around listening to rock-and-roll music on the record player, smoking cigarettes, eating sandwiches or burgers, and chug-a-lugging "Sneaky Pete" wine. Rossi tried to help me fit in with his crowd, but I didn't feel comfortable. Among other things, I was intimidated by the girls. I was attracted to some of them, but I was too bashful to approach them, much less speak to them. The few times I tried, it was a disaster. I made some mumbling comments and then withdrew in embarrassment, scolding myself for sounding so stupid.

So Rossi took me to Kelly's poolroom, several doors away from Johnny's. He knew some of the guys there, and we could shoot pool, he said. I'd never played pool before, but I liked games—any kind of games. They were more fun than being in school or at home.

Kelly's poolroom on Second Street was a place you could hang out with the guys; no women ever went in there. They weren't banned; that's just how things were. If a woman needed her husband, son, or boyfriend for something, she would send another son, or some boy from the neighborhood to go get him.

The poolroom was on the first floor of an old storefront building. The door was one step up off the sidewalk and recessed between large windows that once had displayed merchandise. A tournament-size pool table dominated the room. It was usually dark in there; the door and the venetian blinds over the front windows were kept closed, even during the day. The only light in the room came from a lamp with a funnel-shaped shade hanging over the pool table.

There wasn't much furniture. A black-and-white TV with rabbit ears sat in the right bay of the front window and a few wooden chairs were scattered around the pool table and in front of the TV. Kelly sat behind a small glass counter that held supplies, such as cue tips, chalk, cards, and cigarettes, including Camels and Lucky Strikes. Kelly didn't carry any filter brands, although in those days, before the cigarette health scare, there weren't many filter brands to be had, other than menthol Kools, maybe.

Despite his name, Kelly wasn't Irish. He was 100 percent Polish-American—"Polack," as he liked to say. He was born and raised right there in Elizabeth, New Jersey, and had enlisted in the United States Merchant Marine after high school. The guys in the Merchant Marine couldn't pronounce all those "scz"s in his last name, which was something like "Kelczsinzki," and just started to call him Kelly. It stuck.

After twelve years in the Merchant Marine, he retired with a small injury pension and opened the poolroom. Injury notwithstanding, he was an imposing guy—over two hundred pounds, I guessed. You didn't want to mess with him.

Kelly kept an eye on the players from behind the glass counter and made sure they paid for each game. He was the referee in case of disagreements about the rules and the policeman if arguments broke out. Once in a while, he mellowed out and became a father figure if the younger guys just wanted to sit and talk. When he wasn't watching the pool players, he watched whatever was on the TV, or just dozed off. Some of the guys said he suffered from a form of narcolepsy.

I was hooked on pool from the very first game. I had a burning desire to become good at it. I wasn't good at school; I had no money, few friends, and no girlfriend. Pool offered me a chance to prove myself. Besides, you could make money shooting pool. Every game at Kelly's had some money on it. I was ready to make a killing. But it didn't work out that way. While I got pretty good at it, I wasn't good enough. Some of the guys were *really* good, and it didn't take me long to realize that they were way better than I could ever be.

In the summer, the guys would start showing up at Kelly's early on Saturday mornings. Some of them, like the brothers Joe and Tommy Maiore, would set up a few chairs in the street, turn the radio on to the higher numbers on the AM dial, lean back against the storefront wall, and shoot the breeze about sports, the league they bowled in, girls, or the parties at which they'd gotten drunk the night before. When they heard a song they liked, they'd stop in mid-sentence and sing along. One song that was getting a lot of radio airtime was Bobby Darin's recording of "Mack the Knife." It was tough and *macho,* the way we imagined ourselves to be.

> *Oh, the shark, babe, has such teeth, dear*
> *And it shows them pearly white*
> *Just a jackknife has old MacHeath, babe*
> *And he keeps it...ah...out of sight.*
> *Ya know when that shark bites, with his teeth, babe*

Scarlet billows start to spread
Fancy gloves, though, wears old MacHeath, babe
So there's nevah, nevah a trace of red.

The more intense guys at Kelly's didn't sit outside or sing along with the music. They'd sit inside and gamble on baseball, football, or basketball games on TV. They made bets with each other, or started a money pool if there was a good game on. More often than not, they'd place bets with the bookies or the numbers guys who dropped in from time to time, or play poker in Kelly's back room.

There were two doors at the back of the poolroom: one led to the bathroom and the other to the room where the guys played poker. It was small, not much bigger than a walk-in closet, with no windows. Kelly put a round table in there, big enough to seat six or seven men, if you squeezed, and suspended a 150-watt bulb from the ceiling, just a foot or two above the tabletop. He covered the bulb with an olive-gray funnel shade, like the one above the pool table, to kill the glare.

After graduating from high school, I'd join Kelly and the other guys in the back room once in a while. Friday nights, when most of us got paid, were usually the big ones. We'd cash our paychecks, get a few shots of whiskey, and go to Kelly's looking for action. There'd often be a full table, with another five or six guys standing around, waiting for someone to drop out. The air would be thick with cigarette and cigar smoke but Kelly didn't allow drinking. He drew the line there. He didn't want any liquor-induced fights to break out that would bring the cops. Gambling was illegal, of course, but I'm pretty sure Kelly greased the palms of a few of the regular cops on the beat so they'd look the other way. If things got too rowdy, though, there would be a sharp rap on the street door and Kelly would break up the game.

One Friday night in late October, just before Halloween, the guys gathered at Kelly's early. There were more of us than usual that night and conversations were short. Kelly locked the front door, shut off the light in the poolroom, and we moved to the back.

Seven guys sat down at the table, four or five more stood around, waiting for a chance to get in. Kelly tore the cellophane off a fresh deck of cards and spilled them on to the middle of the table. Joe Maiore scooped them up with both hands, stacked them into a neat pile, separated that into two stacks, and riffled the cards, finishing off each shuffle with a nice bow stack. After several riffle shuffles, he switched the stack to his right hand, rapped the edge against the tabletop, and slapped it face down in front of the player to his right. "Cut," he said.

Mazzi, the player to Joe's right, picked up the top half of the deck and slapped it over to the left.

"Deal me a pair of aces," he announced, holding a stack of bills in his left hand. Mazzi liked to brandish the bills in his left hand, waiting to make an aggressive bet. When his turn came, he'd grab one of the bills with his right hand and slam it down with a flourish. Mazzi wasn't bashful.

Joe placed the bottom of the deck on top of the half cut by Mazzi. "The game is seven-card stud, gentlemen," Joe announced. "The ante is fifty cents. You've got to pay to play."

The players threw their coins into the pot. Some had the right change; some threw in dollar bills and took change from the pot. The ones with bigger bills got change from Kelly, who also served as the banker. Kelly made sure he always had lots of change.

"Pot's right," Joe announced, rapping his right index knuckle on the table twice. He dealt the cards one at a time, spinning them across the table to each player with a flick of his wrist. Joe was good at shuffling and dealing.

"Read 'em and weep; see 'em and sob," he intoned.

Each player was dealt two cards down and one card up. "King is high," Joe announced. "King bets."

Rossi had the king. Like me, he was new to the game, so the old timers had us marked as easy targets.

"Check," he said, squeezing a look at his two down cards. Either his hand was weak, or he'd paired up and was trying to give the impression it was weak. Most of us figured his cards were weak. He worked as a stock boy in a warehouse at the time and didn't earn much.

"Karalius Joe" was to Rossi's right. He was an old timer from Lithuania who loved to play poker. He didn't shoot pool or bet on games; he just liked to play poker. *Karalius* means "king" in Lithuanian and he got the reputation of winning poker hands with a pair of kings.

"You got my king," Karalius Joe said in a thick European accent, looking at Rossi. You could smell the alcohol on his breath. "I play dollar," he said, throwing the bill into the pot.

"Fifty-cent limit!" everyone shouted out. Everyone knew that Karalius Joe knew what the limit was, but it was a ritual he went through whenever he sat down to play poker.

"OK. I play fifty cent," he said taking out his change.

Karalius Joe had only a ten showing, but you could never tell if he was bluffing. He made good money on his job—he had his own contracting business—and he liked to intimidate players with his aggressive betting.

Joe Maiore, with his seven showing, dropped out. He stuck to dealing.

Mazzi was next in line. He had a jack of spades up. "I see your fifty cent and raise you another fifty," Mazzi announced, throwing in a dollar bill from the stack in his left hand. "I don't think you got shit, Karalius."

Karalius's ten did not intimidate Mazzi. Kelly, Tommy Maiore, and I dropped out. John, one of the two "Maverick" brothers, as they liked to call themselves, threw in his dollar. Rossi put his dollar in without saying anything.

"Pot's right," Joe announced again with another rap of his right index-finger knuckle. He dealt cards to the remaining players. Mazzi got a queen and had a jack and a queen showing. Karalius Joe got another ten, for a pair of tens. Rossi got a seven of clubs and had a king/seven showing. Maverick John was dealt an ace to go with his eight.

"Pair of tens bets," Joe said, "but watch out for the ace and eight. Could be a dead man's hand."

Joe knew that the two-pair hand of aces and eights was called "dead man's hand." He said the name came from the hand held by Wild Bill Hickok when he was shot by Jack McCall on August 2, 1876, in Deadwood, South Dakota. McCall was later convicted and hanged for the crime, so I guess there were two dead men from that hand.

"No dead man hand," Karalius Joe announced. "I bet fifty cents."

Rossi and Maverick John called the fifty cents. Mazzi raised it another fifty cents. He must've had two pairs by then. Everyone who was left stayed in.

Joe dealt three more times, twice with up cards and the seventh card down. None of the hands improved on the surface, but everyone stuck it out until the end. After the final betting was over, Karalius Joe turned over his down cards and revealed the third ten. Mazzi had two pairs, queens and jacks. Maverick John had aces and sixes, and Rossi had a pair of kings. Mazzi pushed his cards away in disgust. "You lucky bastard!" he growled at Karalius Joe. "You caught the fucking third ten on the last card."

Karalius Joe raked in the pot money with his large hands. "Baby need shoes," he said with a toothy grin.

Rossi didn't say anything. Kelly took the house cut from the pot before Karalius Joe swept it in. The dealing rotated around the table to the next player, who called the game to be played. It was dealer's choice. Some of the dealers picked draw poker, which was five cards down, betting with each card. Others called five-card stud, "a man's game," like the Maverick brothers of TV fame played. The first card was down, all the others up, and players bet on each card.

When it was my turn to deal, I'd choose the game in which I'd last won a hand, although that didn't happen very often. I played my cards close to the vest and usually dropped out unless I had a good hand early. At least I kept my losses down before I was tapped out.

Rossi played for another half hour that Friday night before he was tapped out. He quit and let someone else take his seat at the table. We found out the next day that Rossi was in jail. The guys from Johnny's said Rossi went to Saint Patrick's Church after he left game and stabbed a nun. The only thing we could figure was that the nun had surprised him as he was trying to get the coins out of the votive candle box. Either that or he was mad about losing his week's pay at the poker game.

CHAPTER 12
CHICAGO

Graduation from high school was a big deal for us. We were done, my DP friends and I, with Thomas Jefferson High School and with the dreariness and agony of academics. We wanted to celebrate the occasion and have an adventure of some sort before settling down to the real world. Our parents didn't have graduation parties for us. The senior prom was a celebration of sorts, although some of us, including me, didn't even have dates. After the prom was over, we went to the farm of a relative of Ray Letkowski and got drunk.

That didn't feel grand enough to mark this rite of passage. By luck, an opportunity came along that summer of 1957. Some Lithuanian DPs decided to have a folk-dance festival at the International Amphitheater in Chicago. There was a long tradition of folk dancing in Lithuania and some of the recent US immigrants got together in an effort to revive it. It was to be the first dance festival since Lithuania lost its independence in World War II and there was a lot of hoopla about it in the Lithuanian-American media.

Mack, Vyto Didzbalis, Ray Bakšys, and I decided to check it out. Dad wasn't happy about that; he wanted me to get a job right away and help support the household. But I wasn't going to be dissuaded; I was eighteen, legally an adult, free of school, and needed to let off some pent-up steam. Besides, with all those young Lithuanians in one place, something exciting was bound to happen.

Spontaneity and inspiration notwithstanding, a few logistics still had to be worked out. First, we didn't belong to any organized dance group, so we'd have to go as spectators. It also meant that we'd have to pick up our own travel and accommodation expenses. Since money was always an issue, we had to be creative.

Vyto Didžbalis had a small Oldsmobile Coupe. If we all chipped in, driving there would be cheaper than flying or taking a bus. And since we didn't have enough money to pay for a hotel, we decided we'd sleep in the car.

We set off early one morning in late June and drove straight through to Chicago without stopping—a distance of about 800 miles. It took us twenty hours. Interstate Route 80 hadn't been built and the roads weren't as good in those days as they are now. We stopped only for oil and gas. The Olds burned a lot of both, especially oil. I think it cost us more for oil than for gas.

I rode in the backseat with Ray Bakšys. It was uncomfortable, especially when we tried to sleep. Public bathrooms in gas stations were good for freshening up, but poor substitutes for a good night's rest. Fortunately, I still didn't have to shave very often.

Twenty-nine dance groups with a total of 1,100 dancers from eighteen US cities performed at the festival. Spectators included thousands of family members, friends, and other Lithuanians. The actual dancing took place in the International Amphitheater on South Halsted Street, adjacent to the Union Stock Yards, where cattle from all over the country were slaughtered and packaged for shipment and sale.

Maybe it was a coincidence, but the Union Stock Yards was the setting for Upton Sinclair's novel, *The Jungle*, in which the fictional Lithuanian immigrant Jurgis Rudkus is exploited and ultimately meets his demise. The novel depicted morbid and unsanitary working conditions, as well as the exploitation of women and children, and caused a sensation when it was published in 1906. The book persuaded Congress to pass federal legislation to regulate the meatpacking industry.

The dance festival, the banquet, and related activities lasted several days. We had enough money to attend the main dance festival, although the price of the tickets for the banquet at the Chicago Hilton on Michigan Avenue was out of our reach. Even if we could've afforded to go, we didn't have any dress clothes. I ran into Jonas Gružauskas, a cousin on my mother's side, in front of the hotel. He had come all the way from Sydney, Australia. He was among those Lithuanians who'd chosen to emigrate to Australia, rather than to the United States. Jonas was tall and athletic and had been a basketball player in his younger years, as well as a coach at the DP camp in Kempten, Allgäu. He remembered my brother, John, to whom he was a role model and mentor of sorts. John often spoke fondly of Jonas, crediting him with inspiring his interest in electrical engineering.

Jonas's story is one of the thousands of untold stories of Lithuanians whose lives were overturned by World War II. He was born in 1922 and was of military age when World War II broke out. Like us, he decided to leave Lithuania with the second Russian occupation in 1944. At age twenty-two, he was a prime candidate for service in the Russian army—if he wasn't killed or sent to Siberia beforehand. He had a beautiful girl-friend in Kaunas and they had plans to marry. He asked her to leave Lithuania with him, but her parents wouldn't allow it. Jonas left without her and, like us, ended up in a DP camp in southern Bavaria, although not the same one.

After immigration became possible, starting in 1949, he decided to go to Australia. On the boat trip to Australia, he met another young woman from Kaunas. They married and had a son in Australia. The son became a doctor. Jonas returned to Lithuania in the early 1970s when it was still occupied by Russia. He visited his sister, Maryte, who had never left Lithuania and met with his onetime love, but all they could do was speculate wistfully about the life they might've had together.

We had slept in the car that first night in Chicago, but it was really cramped. To make it a little more comfortable, the other guys insisted that I contact another distant cousin on my mother's side to see if she would put me up for a night.

My cousin's married name was Strode and she lived in Marquette Park on the South Side of Chicago. She and her family welcomed me into their home when I presented myself to them, but I'm afraid I didn't make a very good impression. The very first night they agreed to put me up, I came back late, about two or three in the morning. Finding the door locked, I climbed in through a partly open window. I didn't want to wake them up and I thought it was the more polite thing to do. The next morning, my cousin's husband was very upset with me. I could feel the cold shoulder as we sat at the dining room table for breakfast. "You're lucky you weren't mistaken for a burglar and shot," he said.

Once the festival was over, the two Vytos decided to drive back to New Jersey. Ray Bakšys and I decided to stay—for a while, at least. I don't know why. We didn't have any other plans, I guess; it was an adventure.

We knew enough to get jobs, though. Ray was hired at a factory right away. I tried several places, including the Chicago Stock Yards, but they weren't hiring. I was somewhat glad about that. The smell of the place was bad, even in the personnel office. My fallback plan was Manpower, the temporary work agency. I wasn't thrilled about working there, but Ray thought it was a good idea. Manpower paid every day and, since Ray wouldn't be paid for a couple of weeks, my temporary work would provide a stream of money to live on in the meantime.

The jobs on which I was sent out every day included digging ditches, unloading freight cars, and other tasks involving manual labor. That part didn't bother me; I was young, healthy, and reasonably strong. The people with whom I had to work made the job tough, though. I was teamed with a "good old boy" from the South, who came in every day with his son. Being bigger and older than I was, the father made sure I did most of the heavy digging and lifting while he and his son "supervised." After a week or so of doing most of the heavy lifting, I couldn't take it anymore. I took a day off, read the want ads, and applied for a job at American National Bank. I was interviewed and hired as a data-entry clerk that same day.

The bank job involved sitting in front of a large adding machine, keying in the dollar amounts of cancelled checks that had been batched for processing, then sorting them into wooden bins above the adding machine, based on the bank routing numbers. The added and sorted checks of each batch had to be reconciled with the original batch totals and then forwarded to the Federal Reserve Bank for re-batching and re-routing to the originating banks.

It was interesting as a learning experience at first, but it didn't take long to become what it really was: boring and tedious. I took comfort in the fact that it was better than digging ditches and unloading freight cars with unpleasant hillbillies.

But then Ray and I still had the problem of cash flow. We ran out of money and Ray wasn't going to be paid until Monday of the following week. By Thursday, we had finished off the last of the food in the fridge. Friday we both worked without eating. Saturday we were both off from work and spent the entire day walking around the South Side of Chicago. We were hoping to run into people we might know.

We didn't. The folk dance festival was over and everyone had left. When we got back to our room, we were exhausted, starved, and desperate—especially Ray. He was so weak he could barely talk. Ray insisted that I go to my cousin in Marquette Park again to see if I could borrow some money. I was reluctant because of the window-climbing incident, but agreed. We were out of options.

Early Sunday morning, I got dressed and started walking to Marquette Park, a distance of more than twenty miles. I didn't have enough money for bus fare. All I had, in fact, was one copper penny. On a lark, I stopped by a scale in front of a drug store and dropped the penny in the slot to weigh myself. The scale stopped at 138, seven pounds less than what I'd weighed just two days earlier.

Even though my stomach was empty, I still had enough energy to get to my destination. Maybe our experience in Germany during the war gave me a reserve. Fortunately, it was sunny and the air was clear after a strong thundershower the night before.

When I arrived at my cousin's house, though, I surmised that there was some sort of an emergency. Everyone was preoccupied and running around. They barely acknowledged my presence. My cousin's son told me that the sump pump had failed and the basement had flooded with last night's thunderstorm. They were carrying furniture and other items out of the basement in an effort to salvage what they could.

I decided it wasn't a good time to hit them up for money. So I swallowed what little saliva I had left and pitched in to help. About noontime, when a semblance of normality was restored, I approached my cousin's son, who was about thirty at the time, and engaged him in conversation. He seemed more sympathetic to me than his Dad, who was still smarting from my window-climbing incident.

I didn't just want to hit him up for a loan without at least a nod to some social graces.

"What kind of work do you do?" I asked politely. He told me he had a regular job, but that he'd figured out how to make a few extra dollars on the side.

"I sell Volkswagen Beetles," he said.

"You mean you work as a car salesman part time?" I asked him.

"No. I buy one and then resell it after it's delivered to me."

I was a little confused. "So why wouldn't somebody buy one from the car dealer?"

"They could," he said, "but then they'd have to wait a year to get it."

He explained that Volkswagen Beetles were becoming very popular in the United States and there was a pent-up demand for them. Since they were only being manufactured in Germany, there was a long wait for delivery—close to a year.

"So I buy one with a small down payment and then sell it after it's delivered. People are willing to pay a premium if they don't have to wait for a year."

This was interesting entrepreneurial stuff to me, but the unrelenting hunger pangs finally gave me the courage to hit him up for a loan.

"Uh, I hate to bring this up," I said, shuffling my feet, "but my friend and I have hit a rough patch. Any chance you could loan us some money?"

He didn't hesitate at all. "Sure," he said. "How much do you need?"

"Can you make it ten dollars?" I didn't dare ask him for more. I would've settled for a five.

He took a small wad out of his pocket and peeled off a ten-dollar bill. I promised to pay him back as soon as we got on our feet, which I did.

My first stop was at a grocery store, where I loaded up a shopping bag with food, including bread, milk, butter, lunchmeat, and a few cookies. (Ten bucks was enough for all that in 1957.) Then I caught a bus back to the Near North Side, eating while I rode. The occasional glances from the other passengers didn't faze me. I was way past any embarrassment. When I arrived at our one-room apartment, Ray was still in bed, almost too weak to eat.

"We got us a feast, Ray," I said, placing the grocery bag on the kitchen table. "Dine away, my friend."

As soon as Ray got some food in his stomach, he threw up. Then he began to nibble on smaller portions and, little by little, regained his strength. By the next morning, he was well enough to go to work and collect his first paycheck. We were back on the gravy train.

Life settled into a routine thereafter. We had food and shelter, but not much else: no family, no friends, and no support system. My desire to be independent ran into the reality of lonesomeness. Ray was more outgoing than I was, and he hooked up with some girls. He brought them over to the apartment a few times and attempted to get me hooked up, too, but it didn't feel right to me. Maybe it was bashfulness, or some sort of idealism; I don't know.

After a few months, Ray decided to go back to New Jersey, at least for a visit. Gloria, his girlfriend back home, had been writing and calling. She wanted him to come back. Ray said he'd visit her and come back in a week. He paid in advance his half of the rent for the week he'd be gone.

Within a few months of returning to Chicago, however, he found out that Gloria was pregnant. He made plans to go back to New Jersey permanently. He left just before Christmas. He married Gloria and had several children thereafter. Ray was a good husband and father, but he continued to drink heavily. Several years later, he got into a bad car accident. He was thrown out of the car and hit his head against a stop sign. When I visited him in the hospital, his swollen head was the size of a watermelon and his right eye seemed to be partly detached. I consoled Gloria as well as I could.

I didn't see much of Ray after that, but the few times I did see him, it was evident that the accident had changed him. I don't know what happened to him in the end, but I'm quite sure he died young.

Back in Chicago, I was left alone for the holidays. It was lonesome, but I didn't want to spend the money to go home. Not that I had much to go home to. Also, I was trying to save up to go to college. I wasn't earning much at the bank, so it was a slow process. I had already applied to Rutgers University in New Brunswick, New Jersey, and was waiting to hear if I had been accepted.

My social life in Chicago wasn't great. I wasn't the social butterfly type to begin with, but I did make some casual acquaintances at the bank and we socialized after work from time to time. We'd go to restaurants or movies and then finish up with some sightseeing. One time we decided to go to the top of the forty-one-story Prudential building, the tallest skyscraper in Chicago at the time. Our ears popped as we were whisked up to the top in the elevator.

Some of my coworkers were my age; others were older. Some, I learned, were gay. For the first time in my life, I was introduced to—confronted by might be a better description—some parts of the gay culture. Herman, a fellow bank employee, took a liking to me and wanted to hang around with me. He was born and raised in Minnesota and was about twenty-eight at the time. On one of our group outings, he didn't leave even after the group split up for the evening. I lived close to the downtown area, on the Near North Side, and, under the circumstances, felt obligated to act as the host. I invited him to a local bar for a nightcap, thinking that we would have one more drink before he took the bus back to his place.

It didn't work out that way. For starters, he was acting weird, I thought. He had a dreamy look about him and played "It Had to Be You," on the jukebox. I don't remember if it was the Peggy Lee rendition, or Julie London's, but it was sultry. I was socially naïve and, when we discovered it was too late for him to catch a bus, I invited him to spend the night with me. I finally got the gist of what he was about when he tried to put his arm around me in the one bed I had.

"Stop that!" I shouted at him. "I don't do that!"

When he persisted, I shouted at him again. "Either you stop that or I'll punch you and throw you out of the bed!"

He behaved the rest of the night, but I couldn't sleep a wink. I was too upset and confused about what had just happened. I don't think he slept, either. We went to work the next day like walking zombies. That misunderstanding ended whatever casual relationship we'd had. He continued to hang around with the group, but he never made another pass at me. Whenever I glanced at him, his eyes would glow with shame and he would try to avoid looking back at me.

I felt sorry for him. At the time, I didn't really understand the deep feelings and conflicts that seemed to be burning inside him. In those days, being gay carried an enormous stigma and most gays remained in the closet. This personal conflict placed a heavy emotional burden on him. If I had the burden of not knowing who I was, Herman and other gays had the burden of knowing who they were but not being able to be themselves. They acted out their sexual identities in bedrooms, in public bathhouses, or even back alleys. That was before the human immunodeficiency virus unleashed the AIDs epidemic.

Then there was Henry, another coworker. He was older, perhaps forty at the time, and hailed from Austria. He didn't act like a "flaming" gay and you couldn't tell he was gay by looking at him. He kept inviting me to come to his place for dinner. He said he was a very good cook and would prepare a meal of my choice.

I didn't really see him as a friend, but the offer of a home-cooked meal was tempting. I finally agreed one day and suggested chicken vegetable soup. It was every bit as good as he had promised and I felt content and relaxed afterwards. It felt almost like home. He was a gracious host and suggested I recline on the couch, which I did. That's when he kneeled down alongside the couch and attempted to unzip my fly. I bolted into alertness and told him that I didn't do that. To his credit, he made no effort to continue. His self-control was admirable, but what trust I had in him as a father figure of sorts was broken. I left his apartment shortly thereafter.

Sometimes I'd go to see a movie by myself. One time I walked into a theater that, apparently, was a hangout for gays. I didn't realize it and walked into the bathroom after the movie was over. A row of men stood at the urinals as if they were in a lineup at the police station. They were waiting for some sort of a signal. I felt ten pairs of eyes fixed on me as I did my business and then made the mistake of making eye contact with one of the men on my way out. He followed and attempted to make a connection. I declined politely and hurried off.

There was one more gay incident after that. Gordon, one of my new roommates, invited me to a cocktail party. After Ray Bakšys moved back to New Jersey, I hooked up with Mike, another bank employee. He was a nice young man who had a place at 5201 Dorchester Street in Hyde Park. His parents had moved to California, but he wanted to remain in Chicago. They let him stay in their house, provided he made payments on the mortgage. He subleased the place to other people so he could afford to keep it. I was one of them.

I had to share a bed with Gordon, who was a very restless sleeper. He would talk in his sleep and jump up frequently, as if he were having nightmares. When I asked him about his nightmares, he avoided the subject and tactfully made me feel that I was transgressing a private zone. I wasn't used to that type of diplomatic nicety.

Gordon was in his late twenties or early thirties, and had been a Catholic priest. I never got a straight answer from him as to why he left the religious life. I was starting to lose my naiveté and suspected that he was also gay, though he never made a pass at me. But he's the one who invited me to a cocktail party that was attended by men only. Many of them seemed to know Gordon, but it was definitely not a traditional stag party. There were no cards, cigars, or raunchy humor at the expense of women. I think many of them were his friends from the seminary.

I felt out of place and proceeded to get totally smashed on vodka and orange juice. The drinks tasted like orange juice and I just kept downing them. After I began to loosen up and slur my speech, several men offered to take me home. Fortunately, Gordon rescued me from my drunken innocence and took me back to the apartment in a cab.

Mike was straight, and one of my better friends. I trusted him. He was a quiet, unassuming guy, though somewhat on the nerdy side. He was not very athletic and had flat feet, although that didn't keep him from getting drafted into the army some time after I returned to New Jersey. He had another friend, Joe, who was a teller at the bank. Joe was tall and lanky, and had a casual, friendly manner about him. The three of us hung out from time to time.

Joe and Mike were into jazz, especially from the swing era. They liked Benny Goodman, the king of swing; Tommy Dorsey, Artie Shaw, and Paul Whiteman, as well as notable musicians like Charlie Christian, Jack Teagarden, and Louis Armstrong. Joe had a large collection of vinyl singles and LPs, including Artie Shaw's 1938 RCA label release of the American classic, "Begin the Beguine," composed by Cole Porter, and one or more versions of Hoagy Carmichael's composition, "Stardust."

The creative process involved in the composition of music, especially jazz, also fascinated them. One of their favorite recordings was from an impromptu jam session in March 1941 of Benny Goodman's sextet, which included Charlie Christian, a black musician who was one of the first to play an electrically amplified guitar. They were waiting for Benny Goodman to show up and started to riff by way of killing time.

The sound engineers had turned on the microphones to test the equipment and recorded the twenty-minute session. They later reduced it to about six minutes and released it with the name "Waiting for Benny." While it was never popular with the public, it became an underground hit among the jazz cognoscenti.

I found out later, incidentally, that Benny Goodman was born in Chicago, the ninth of twelve children of poor Jewish immigrants from the Russian Empire. His father, David Goodman, was a tailor from Warsaw, Poland, and his mother was Dora Grinsky from Kaunas, Lithuania. I thought that was an interesting connection.

But in spite of the harsh realities of living as an immigrant, and in spite of my struggles with identity and self-confidence, my dream was to make it in America. One of the first things I wanted to do when I turned eighteen was to become a US citizen. My parents had already become citizens after the mandatory five-year waiting period. My younger brother, Henry, and my sister, Maria, became citizens automatically when my parents did because they were minors. I was over sixteen, but less than eighteen, so I had to wait until I became a legal adult.

I applied for and received my certificate of naturalization from the Clerk of the US District Court for the Northern District of Illinois on July 29, 1958. I remember being quizzed by the judge's Clerk, who asked the usual softball questions.

"Who is the president of the United States?" he asked me, somewhat routinely.

"Dwight D. Eisenhower," I answered confidently. Noticing my confidence and the lack of any accent, he gave me a slight glance.

"How often is the president elected?" he went on.

"Every four years, sir."

When he realized that I seemed reasonably knowledgeable, he smiled and asked if I knew what the twenty-second amendment to the Constitution, which had been ratified by the states several years earlier, was all about.

"It limits the terms of the president to two four-year terms," I answered proudly.

He shook my hand and handed me my certificate of naturalization.

As part of the citizenship procedure, my parents and two younger siblings had changed their surnames from "Monkevičius" to "Mankus." I liked Mankus, too. It sounded more American, although it retained its Lithuanian roots, I thought. I also was tired of spelling "Monkevičius" repeatedly at the cleaners, on the phone, in school, and at the many other places where that issue came up. Finally, the repeated and often deliberate butchering of my last name by other kids had left me with negative feelings about it.

I had the same problem with my first name, Algimantas. So I changed t to Anthony. My second given name was Antanas, which is Lithuanian for Anthony, so it wasn't a big stretch. But I wasn't too fond of Anthony, either; it sounded too formal to me. So I eventually changed it legally to Tony.

To make things more confusing, my oldest brother, John, had changed his surname to "Monkvic" when he got his citizenship while serving in the Air Force. My other brother, Ray, never became a citizen and never changed his name legally, so he still goes by Monkevičius, although he pronounces is as if it were spelled "Monkvic."

I know, it doesn't make much sense, but that's not an uncommon subtext of the immigrant experience. Years ago when Lithuanian immigrants were processed through Ellis Island, their surnames were often misunderstood or mispronounced, so the immigration officials Americanized them in the records. Failing that, they "Polandized" the Lithuanian names because they were more familiar with Polish names, thus frustrating future generations of genealogists.

Notwithstanding the good feeling I got from becoming a citizen, I was lonesome all the time in Chicago. I could also see that I didn't have much of a future at the bank. Even though I dreaded the thought of more formal education, I decided to try college.

I was accepted at Rutgers, packed up my things, and flew back to New Jersey the following month, the first time I had ever flown an airplane. It was the dawn of commercial jet aviation, but my plane was powered by dual-piston engines. Compared with my trip to Chicago a year earlier in the Oldsmobile coupe, this was a luxury. The flight attendants were still called stewardesses then, and they had to be single and pretty.

As I winged out of Chicago from Midway Airport (O'Hare hadn't been built yet), I cast a wistful good-bye glance out the window. It had been my first foray into independent adulthood and I felt a bittersweet sense of longing, mixed with a vague feeling of remorse. As the plane arced gradually into the vast, open sky, my thoughts turned to dreams for the future. At the time, I couldn't know that not only would I return to Chicago, but that I would settle permanently in its suburbs in the second half of my peripatetic life.

CHAPTER 13
THE REAL WORLD

Rutgers University is located on a beautiful campus in New Brunswick, next to the Raritan River. It was chartered as Queen's College in November 1766 to "educate the youth in language, liberal, the divinity, and useful arts and sciences," making it one of the oldest colleges in the United States. It was an all-male institution until 1970 when the board of governors voted to admit women. In September 1958, I moved into a dorm with three other young men and started the basic courses that all freshmen were required to take, like physics, math, and English composition.

The rich history and the idyllic setting of the campus notwithstanding, I failed all of my courses and dropped out after one semester. My young brain was not wired for academics. In the academic world, you sit in a classroom and listen to polite lectures on abstract topics, and after class, you read books about them; you don't do the rough-and-tumble things I did to survive in my early years.

My first stab at higher education was a complete failure. I don't remember much about the experience, except for the strong feeling that I didn't belong there. I moved back in with my parents in Elizabeth and began looking for a job. I wasn't happy about being dependent on Mom and Dad again, but there was a roof over my head and food on the table. Survival trumped pride.

I didn't have a plan for the future, other than getting a job, any job. Income was the bottom line for survival. I thought I would work during the day, sign up for some night courses at a local college, and start working toward a degree on a part-time basis. The Newark campus of Rutgers offered that option and I enrolled there eventually, taking one or two courses per semester.

I found a job at a local bank in Elizabeth doing pretty much the same thing I did at the bank in Chicago. I had started on an employment track as a drone in the check-processing department and that seemed to be my role in life for the foreseeable future.

Then I got a break—or thought I did. It was the dawn of the computer age and banks were in the forefront of this revolution. Our bank was looking to automate many of its operating functions, including the check processing that was being done semi-manually in my department. The comptroller of the bank, who was supervising the project, signed a contract to buy a large GE computer along with peripheral equipment, such as high-speed readers/sorters, printers, and magnetic tape drives, in order to make the process more efficient and less costly. He built a separate building to house the computer and the peripheral equipment. In those days, a computer took up an entire room and needed a large HVAC unit to handle the heat generated by the multiple rows of transistors.

He then decided to staff the newly created automation department with current employees. He knew absolutely nothing about computers or programming, but he was old school and saw merit in shifting lower-paid current employees to the new department rather than hiring expensive programmers with technical expertise. That decision came back to haunt him eventually.

I took a test and scored highly enough to be offered one of the programmer positions. I joined the staff along with two other employees, a supervisor from the check-processing department, my former boss; and a teller. John, a nice young man who was the only one in our department with several years of programming experience, supervised us.

The job was fun at first and I had hopes that this would be a career path for me. I had my own office with a desk—which was a big deal to me—and responsibility for a larger project. This was much better than the repetitive, brainless tasks to which I was accustomed. I was put on salary, rather than hourly pay, and that carried a certain amount of prestige. We even had a group secretary. She was older, but still attractive. She was respectful to us and made us feel like executives.

After the newness and the glamour wore off, though, the hard job of programming began. One of the problems was that the bank had chosen to go with General Electric, a GE-210-E computer, rather than IBM equipment. IBM had the most experience in the field at the time and offered good hardware and some pre-packaged software, in addition to good technical support. GE was new to the field and offered no pre-packaged software. That meant that we had to write all programs ourselves, including the most basic ones, like read and write commands, as well as print commands. We also had to write the programs using the compiler assembly program, one of the most rudimentary programming languages at the time. It was just one step above binary code. GE must've offered the bank a more competitive financial package. I guess that made sense to the penny-pinching comptroller, although it turned out to be penny wise and pound foolish.

The programming was tedious and time consuming. I can't say I enjoyed it, nor was I exceptionally good at it. But the pay was better and the work more interesting than what I had done in the check-processing department. So I drank ten or twelve cups of coffee a day and pushed myself to keep going. I wrote some programs that worked, so I think I did a credible job, considering my lack of experience in programming, but I wasn't a born programmer. I had to rack my brain to get things right.

Some people, I found out, were much better at it. That fact was brought home to me on one occasion when we decided to test our skills with a game. It involved writing a program to test the accuracy of the high-speed magnetic check reader/sorter. Checks that came in to the bank were magnetically encoded with the bank routing number, the account number, and the dollar amount. These checks were bundled into stacks and fed through the high-speed check reader/sorter, which had an electronic sensor that could "read' the manually encoded magnetic numbers. Since some of the magnetic numbers were defectively encoded or worn out through handling, the sorter/reader would either not recognize them or misread them. To help spot any misreads in the account number, the last digit of the account number was always a "check digit" whose purpose was to verify the accuracy of the check reader by a mathematical formula. We had to write a program that would manipulate the account numbers in a certain way to come up with the number shown in the check digit. If the result didn't match the check digit, the check would be sent to an error bin and had to be recoded.

The mathematical formula was simple. You doubled each digit and if the result was more than nine, you added the two digits together. After that, the program added all the numbers together and compared the last digit of the result to the check digit. If it was a match, you knew you had a good read; if not, the check had to be sent to a separate bin for recoding.

The game we decided to play was to see who could write a program to do the check-digit verification with the least number of programming instructions, and therefore in the shortest amount of time. The three of us programmers, plus the supervisor, John, came up with routines that did that with more or less the same number of instructions. The difference between our routines was minimal.

But then came along Ray Letkowski, my friend from Second Street and Johnny's restaurant. He had recently graduated from Villanova University with a degree in math and, at my recommendation, was hired by the bank to join our programming group. He took up the check-digit challenge only weeks after being hired and wrote a routine that was simpler, faster, and more elegant than any of those that we more experienced programmers had come up with. That's when it dawned on me that, in the long run, my future wouldn't be in programming.

Apart from the games, though, this automation project was in trouble from the start. By the third year, we were hopelessly behind schedule, and there was no end in sight. The comptroller brought in the consultant from GE who had worked with us from time to time to be with us on a full-time basis. John, our experienced supervisor, saw the writing on the wall and quit for another job. I saw the ship listing badly and thought I'd better do something, too.

I contacted an employment agency and worked with a nice woman who suggested that I take a two-week vacation from the bank and sign up for a programming course with IBM. She said the IBM 1401 computer was becoming very popular and there were numerous jobs available in that field.

Just before I was scheduled to take my vacation, the comptroller called me into his office and instructed me to cancel or postpone my vacation.

"I can't have you take the vacation now," he said. "I need you to work with the GE consultant during this transition period."

"But I have made plans already," I pleaded.

"You'll have to change them," he said with finality.

I was in a quandary about what to do. I had already signed up for the two-week course with IBM and paid the fee. I stood to lose the tuition if I cancelled now, or changed the date. I asked for advice from the woman at the employment agency and she said I should take the vacation and the course. That's when the comptroller fired me.

I took the two-week course and passed it, but I couldn't get another programming job. Any future employer who called the bank for a reference was given a very negative appraisal of my work. Employers were all-powerful in those days; the legal concept of wrongful discharge hadn't been recognized yet. You either conformed to the corporate culture, as exemplified by IBM (affectionately known as "Big Blue"), or you were ostracized.

Sure, there was a small counterculture movement of nonconformists, known as Beatniks, who bucked this culture. Allen Ginsberg, the openly gay poet and activist, wrote radical slam poetry like "Howl." Jack Kerouac's book *On the Road* articulated the nagging thoughts of many corporate men who longed to assert their individuality. But while I read about them with some fascination, I was never truly drawn to that lifestyle. Like most men of my age at that time, I was part of the Silent Generation and toed the line. It was still the post-World War II era of the *Organization Man* and *The Man in the Gray Flannel Suit,* and I aspired to blend into that culture.

Not having any other realistic option, I accepted the dismissal and the blackballing. In the end, it was probably a blessing since I was never cut out to be a programmer geek. In the short run, though—if you call the next four or five years a short run—it was a disaster. I went from one job to another, each one seemingly worse than the last. For a while, I worked with subcontractors who shingled homes for a living. One of them was the older brother of Vyto Didžbalis. He and his other brother were responsible, strong, and hardworking, especially the oldest one, who had overall responsibility for the business. He already had a wife and some young children and seemed to have his feet on the ground.

We set up scaffolding, in good weather or bad, and nailed shingles onto new homes. There was always pressure to work faster because earnings depended on efficiency. I still have a souvenir from those days: a scar on my right hand from when my knife slipped and the edge of a shingle tore open the skin between my thumb and the index finger.

But the job was repetitious and mind-numbing. Some winter days, when the weather was too inclement, we'd recess for lunch to a local bar and never go back. Of course, we didn't get paid for the R&R time, although the older Didžbalis usually bought the first few rounds.

After a while, I was forced to quit the shingling job because of an allergy to vegetation. Due to a deviated septum (a souvenir from a fight with one of the guys from Johnny's Restaurant), the mucus produced by my allergy during summer months wouldn't drain properly and I would get ear, nose, and throat infections requiring antibiotic treatment.

So I tried bartending for a while. I got a job at Lithuanian Liberty Hall, the same place where I used to shine shoes and set pins at the four bowling alleys after I turned sixteen. It was disheartening. Serving drinks to Lithuanian sots didn't live up to my expectations for myself. I remember one elderly gentleman in particular. He was about eighty-five years old and would come in almost every night and sit by himself for several hours. He usually ordered three or four rye whiskey shots during the course of the evening and by the time he drank the third one, he would be crying.

"What's wrong, Jurgis," I asked one night. "Why are you crying?"

"It's my horse," he said, wiping the tears from his eyes. "I loved that horse."

"What happened to it?" I asked sympathetically.

"I had to leave it when we left Lithuania. I couldn't take it with us."

Then there was Dominick, the general manager of LLH. He would go through alcoholic mood swings from time to time. That was no fun.

After a while, my youthful optimism and energy began to wane. It began to dawn on me that the "real world" wasn't fun. The powerful events of my early years in Europe that had dictated my life were over; my childhood in the United States, where my parents and schools laid out the agenda for me, was over. I was now an adult living in a free society and had to take charge of my life.

The only problem was I didn't know how to do that. I knew enough to get jobs so I could at least support myself, but the jobs I got were not what I had in mind for my future.

Why couldn't I be more like my brother, John, I asked myself more than once. John had joined the Air Force long ago and was now an officer and a pilot. He was doing what he loved and making a good living at it. He made succeeding in America seem easy. I know it wasn't. I know he worked very hard to accomplish what he did. The Army drafted him during the Korean War, but he chose to enlist in the Air Force instead, even though it meant an additional two years of obligatory service. John wanted to fly.

Even as a youngster, he loved airplanes. He built a scale model of a fighter plane out of balsa wood when we lived in Germany. It took him weeks to glue all the pieces together and decal it with the appropriate insignia. A rubber band powered the propeller. After John finished it, we scampered up to the fifth floor of the *lager* building. John lofted it softly out the fifth-floor window and we watched his work of love glide into the airspace above the camp. It soared beautifully for a while and then plummeted and crashed to the ground.

We were heartbroken. After all the buildup and the anticipation, it was a big letdown. But maybe it wasn't a failure in the bigger scheme of things. During those weeks leading up to the flight, we had lived in a heightened sense of anticipation. We'd had a feeling of hope during those days, hope that had made us come alive—at least for a while.

After he enlisted in the Air Force, John was trained to be an airplane mechanic. As he recalled it later, he'd service a plane and hang around waiting for the pilot to take it up. When the pilot showed up, John would help him into the cockpit and ask him how it felt to be airborne. The pilot would get a distant gaze, John said, and tell him that there was no other feeling like it in the world.

After a while, John was promoted to jet-fighter crew chief. But he kept striving toward his goal of becoming a pilot. He took college cours-es at night and applied for the Aviation Cadet Commissioning Program. He was accepted into the program and successfully completed flight training. In December 1954, he earned his wings and received his commission as a second lieutenant. After advanced flight training in Florida, he became a pilot and was assigned to a fighter squadron in California. He flew the new jet fighters that had been developed after World War II and served in Japan and other places, including two tours of combat duty in Vietnam.

Me, I was still hanging around Kelly's at the time. Kelly's poolroom offered an escape from the boredom of my daily existence, but I had mixed feelings about it. The books and magazines I read, the movies and TV programs I saw, the people I met—at least some of them—told me there was more to life. I subscribed to *Time* magazine and read every issue from cover to cover. I thought it was important to know what was going on in the world. I even saved the back issues, for some reason. At one point, I had several hundred of them stacked on the floor in my bedroom.

Don't get me wrong, I liked some of the guys at Kelly's. I liked Tommy Maiore, for example, the younger brother of Joe Maiore. They were both regulars there. Tommy was a good listener.

"What are your plans for the future?" I asked Tommy one Saturday morning. It was a sunny spring day and the door to Kelly's poolroom was open to let in some fresh air. The TV was on, but it was too early for any sporting events so no one was paying attention to it.

"Well, I've got a wife and two children, so I have to take care of them," Tommy answered, not sure of where I was heading. "What about you?"

"I'm not sure," I answered. "I just know that I want to get away from here. I feel like I'm in a rut."

"Well, you have to have some idea of where you want to go; have a plan, maybe."

"I know. I tried but I can't come up with one."

"What are you good at? What do you like to do?"

"I like to travel. Maybe I could go into the foreign service."

"I think you need a college degree for that. Even then, I think it's mostly for the rich. You have to have connections to get into that."

"Maybe I could be a writer," I said. "I like to write."

"C'mon, Tony; I like you, but you sound like a dreamer."

"Well, what about you? Don't you have any dreams?"

"Look around you. What do you see? Do you see a big, bright future around here?"

"That's what I mean. That's why I'd like to get out of here."

"I graduated from the Thomas Edison High School, a vocational trade school. I know what's possible for me and I've accepted that."

"But I don't want to accept that; I want more."

"How are you going to get that? You're an immigrant kid from a poor family living in Elizabeth, New Jersey. What are your chances?"

At best, Tommy thought I was an unrealistic dreamer; at worst, an elitist snob who wanted to be better than others in the neighborhood were.

I felt badly about that. I didn't want to be a dreamer, or a snob. For better or worse, I had an idealistic vision of the world, and probably a naïve one. Maybe I should've just kept my mouth shut.

CHAPTER 14
WHO AM I?

One of the other things that added to my self-doubt was the issue of identity: I wasn't sure who I was. Being an immigrant, I was conflicted about my cultural identity. Was I a Lithuanian, an American, or a Lithuanian-American? I felt a kinship to all three groups, but sometimes those identities seemed to conflict.

On the surface, my Lithuanian identity was the strongest. I had the Lithuanian roots going for me and the desire to be part of the Lithuanian culture in which I had grown up. Mom and Dad were the strongest link to that part. They spoke Lithuanian at home and had a number of Lithuanian friends. They read Lithuanian newspapers and attended Lithuanian social and cultural functions, such as concerts, commemorations of Lithuanian independence, church picnics, etc. They encouraged us kids to maintain our roots.

But they spent a lot of time talking about Baisogala, the village where they were raised, the people they had known, and the relatives they left behind. I was sympathetic to all that, but those things didn't have much meaning for me. I didn't really know the people they talked about and had only vague recollections of Lithuania beyond the narrow childhood world I remembered. I wanted to speak of the present and the future, not the past. But they—especially Dad—spoke disparagingly and critically of American culture, a culture I admired and aspired to join. I aspired to what I saw on television, to what I read in the newspapers and magazines, to what I saw around me, especially in the nicer neighborhoods. I didn't want to follow in Dad's footsteps; he didn't seem to have much respect among Americans, or even among his Lithuanian peers, for that matter.

And then he went on those drinking binges. What kind of a role model was that? Of course, I realize now how tough life was for him, how little he'd had to look forward to. The culture and identity he grew up with in Lithuania meant little in America; he was marginalized here. Notwithstanding that, he worked very hard to provide for his family—for a better future for his kids. After a while, though, the dreariness and monotony of his work, the bleakness of his future, and the physical weariness he felt after work every day would overwhelm him. He would deal with those feelings the only way he knew how, the only way he could: by getting smashed out of his brain.

Did it solve his problems? No, but he was able to escape, to forget temporarily, before he went back to more of the same. A good drinking binge revived his psyche and restored his sense of motivation to go on. Thank God for his physical strength. His body recovered from the physical abuse of drinking, at least when he was still relatively young. It became less resilient as he got older.

Then there were the apartments we lived in. The first one, at the boarded-up storefront below Aunt Eva's place on Front Street, was just a few steps away from the water's edge at the confluence of Newark Bay and the Kill Van Kull tidal strait. On the east side of Newark Bay was Bayonne. In the summer, when the wind was right, a terrible smell, like something decomposing, wafted across the bay. Some people said it was from a soap factory in Bayonne. On the southeast side, across the Arthur Kill, was Staten Island where we went drinking with fake IDs once we turned sixteen or so.

We stayed in that apartment for a month or so, until Mom and Dad earned enough for a better place. Mom went to work with Aunt Eva at the umbrella factory the day after we came ashore in New York Harbor. She got her first paycheck within two weeks and, with the help of a loan from Aunt Eva, she saved up enough for a deposit and the first month's rent for a real apartment.

Although an immigrant family of eight with five children wasn't a very desirable tenant for any landlord, we did manage to find a three-bedroom apartment on the third floor of a building on Inslee Place, just a few blocks from Saints Peter and Paul Church. The landlord was never very happy with us, though. We made a lot of noise and provoked frequent complaints from the family below. We were often late with the rent payments, especially when Dad drank away his paycheck. After a few years, the landlord refused to renew our lease.

We found another place on the corner of Fulton and First Streets, two floors above a tavern. On Friday and Saturday nights, the jukebox in the tavern was turned way up and it would be hard to sleep. Sometimes the bar customers would get rowdy and start to argue or fight. Police would be called to restore order. We lived there for six or seven years.

Finally, Mom and Dad saved enough money for a down payment on a home on Madison Avenue. It was close to a hundred years old when we bought it, but it had a small front yard and a bigger one in the back. It wasn't luxurious by any stretch of the imagination, but it was located in a residential area with some trees and, most importantly, it was out of the port area where we had been stuck for years. It was a good thing Dad loved to putter around fixing things because there was never a shortage of things to fix. Mom planted vegetables in a garden she made in the backyard. We even had a dog for a while, although he was high-strung and would mess up Mom's garden by digging holes.

The places we lived were not like the ones I saw on television or in magazines. That added to my desire to get out of the house. John was in the Air Force and was long gone. We hardly ever saw him anymore. Ray also had enlisted in the Air Force and stayed in for five or six years. After he came back, he stayed in the house briefly, but then he got married and moved away. I wanted to get out, too.

The Lithuanian DP boys with whom I hung out were the other part of my Lithuanian identity, but it didn't seem like they were headed for success, either. Several of them, including Vyto Didžbalis and Ray Bakšys, became heavy drinkers as they got older. Not having anything better to do, I would join them from time to time. After the age of seventeen, I forged the birthdate on my driver's license. In those days, the drivers' licenses were printed on soft cardboard. A clerk at the state motor vehicle bureau typed in the driver's name, address, and date of birth. It didn't take a lot of skill to alter the last digit on the year of my birth (1939) from a nine to an eight. We then took the ferry to Staten Island, where the drinking age was eighteen. The bartenders checked our IDs, but not very carefully.

We would binge on beer and/or shots of whiskey until two or three in the morning. There were a number of bars along the bus route in Staten Island and we would stop at one or another, or sometimes a series of them. We would order pitchers of beer and play games that required the loser to chugalug a glass of beer. As the evening wore on, we'd dunk shot glasses of Seagram's 7 whiskey in the beer and down them together. To add to the entertainment, we'd smoke cigarettes and drop coins in the jukebox. Fats Domino was big at the time and we'd sing along with him as the jukebox belted out some of his greatest hits: "Ain't that a Shame," "Blueberry Hill," "I'm in Love Again," "I'm Walkin'," and "Blue Monday." I also liked Guy Mitchell, who had a number of hit singles in that era, including "Singing the Blues," "Sparrow in the Treetop," and "The Roving Kind."

We'd drink until the bars closed, usually at two or three in the morning. One night of the week—either Friday or Saturday—the bars would stay open until four in the morning. Throwing up at the bar, or on the bus ride home, wasn't uncommon. I'd stumble home at five or six in the morning and crawl into bed. One time I awoke around noon and saw crud all over the covers. I didn't know what it was at first. Then I figured out that I had vomited in my sleep without waking up.

I was lucky I didn't choke. They say God loves children and drunks. At that point, I had both going for me.

The Lithuanian DP girls in the neighborhood were also part of my social circle. Some of them were pretty, I thought, and I had crushes on a few of them. But they didn't seem to like me. They probably considered me too immature and lacking the aspiration to better my social status. They were right about my immaturity.

They belonged to Scout troops and/or other Lithuanian student organizations. I joined some of those groups several times, but didn't seem to fit in. My sense of social interaction consisted of horseplay and rough-housing, something the girls—and some of the more mature guys—didn't think much of. Also there was a social pecking order among the Lithuanian DPs. It was based, in part, on who their parents had been in the old country. Many of them had been educated and had held respectable jobs in Lithuania, even if they were forced to work in less glamorous ones after they came to America. By that measure, my parents and I were near the bottom.

The second part of my identity at that time was my Lithuanian-American one. I belonged to several organizations that included second- or third-generation Lithuanian-Americans. Their parents or grandparents had emigrated from Lithuania, but they had been born in the United States and were already "Americanized." Some held better jobs, had acquired property, and had a wider support system. They didn't feel as conflicted about the two cultures as I did. Many of them viewed their Lithuanian roots simply as a social connection to people with similar backgrounds.

I got to know many of them through the Knights of Lithuania and the Rūta Ensemble. The Knights of Lithuania was founded in 1913 by the first wave of Lithuanian immigrants. From the beginning, its members organized political, religious, and social activities. The Newark Chapter, to which I belonged on and off, hosted or participated in several events each year, including the annual commemoration of Lithuania's first declaration of independence on February 16, 1918. It also had a bowling league. Since I enjoyed sports, I joined and even served as its executive secretary for several years.

Dottie Dutkus was the secretary of the Newark chapter at that time. She never married and was already in her forties or fifties, but she was fun to be with and enjoyed social activities. Her nephew, a big, strong, young man, was a New Jersey State trooper. He joined us from time to time. Connie Mack and her sister, Gloria, were also among the regulars. They were cousins of Marty Rusgis, who was the most outgoing of the bunch and the life of most parties. I liked Connie. Even though she was older than I was, she was always good for a squeeze and a kiss, especially after a few drinks.

Finally, there was Larry Janonis, who was a regional officer with the Knights of Lithuania. He was largely integrated into the American society and had a good job. He and his wife had no children, but entertained often, especially at their summer home in Shirley, Long Island. The whole gang would go there for weekends. He had a good bar and plenty of food. After the party got going, he would put on some records and ask us to sing along. He was especially fond of Tony Bennett's recording of "San Francisco." He wasn't happy until we did a full-throated rendition of the finale, ending with:

> *"When I come home to you, San Francisco, Your golden sun will shine for me."*

Fortunately, we were too drunk to notice how awful that must have sounded.

Jack Stukas, a second-generation Lithuanian-American who had a weekly radio program called "Memories of Lithuania" founded the Rūta Ensemble. His show was broadcast in Lithuanian an AM radio station that catered to ethnic audiences. The format consisted of music, interviews with Lithuanian personalities, announcements of local cultural events, and some light news. Jack was outgoing and generally liked by the Lithuanians in the New Jersey/New York area. Eventually, he earned a PhD and became president of a small savings and loan association in Carteret, New Jersey, although he died at a relatively young age.

Rūta Ensemble was a choral group that sang Lithuanian folk songs, although its repertoire also included operatic numbers. We performed mostly at local Lithuanian concerts, although periodically we would be invited to perform for other Lithuanian communities outside of New Jersey, and even recorded some LPs. The group was a mixture of Lithuanian DP immigrants and second- and third-generation Lithuanian-Americans. I was actively involved with the group for a numbers of years, and made some friends there. Val Melinis was the president of Rūta Ensemble for many years. His mother, two brothers, and his sister, Mary, also belonged to the group. His mother had a beautiful mezzo soprano voice and was part of a spinoff quartet with Mrs. Kidžius, together with their respective daughters, Mary (Marytė) Melinis and Ilene Kidzius. The Melinises and the Kidziuses were DPs like me, although their grandchildren were born in the United States.

During the period I belonged to the group, Florence Schirm, a second-generation Lithuanian who was married to Matt Schirm, usually sang the female solo parts. Florence had a rich and powerful mezzo soprano voice and was a good friend of mine. She and Matt had four children. Lou Stukas, a baritone and the brother of Jack Stukas, often sang the male solos. Algirdas Kačanauskas directed the choir. He was well into his fifties at the time and a heavy drinker. His legs had sores, probably from diabetes. His father had been a well-known composer and musician in Lithuania. After rehearsals at the Lithuanian church in Newark, or at Lithuanian Liberty Hall in Elizabeth, he and most of the group would convene to the bar where he would proceed to gossip, talk dirty, and feel up some of the older DP women. They seemed to be tolerant, even admiring in some cases, of his ribald personality and the "naughty boy" image he cultivated. It provided a modicum of excitement in their otherwise ordinary lives. Like him, some of the older Lithuanian DP women were single or had lost their husbands during the war. They probably realized that he was mostly bark and little bite, although who knew what might have gone on behind closed doors, especially when they were younger.

I enjoyed some of the activities of these two groups, especially traveling to the annual conventions of the Knights of Lithuania or performing concerts with the Rūta Ensemble. It took me out of my head and helped me to interact socially. In the long run, though, I still felt that these groups were dead ends. Even when I was enjoying myself, I kept trying to figure out how to escape that environment.

So I was conflicted about my Lithuanian and Lithuanian-American identities and kept reaching out to the larger American culture. But my American identity was even vaguer. It was represented mostly by what I saw around me on television, in newspapers and magazines, and in school. It was more of a goal than tangible reality. The actual American kids with whom I hung out weren't much as role models, either. They weren't like the ones I saw on TV or read about in the newspapers and magazines. They were kids at Thomas Jefferson High School or in Kelly's Poolroom on Second Street. I really didn't feel close to any of them, though some were friendlier to me than others were.

Ray Letkowski was one person who didn't put me down. Besides having some classes together in high school, I would see him on Second Street from time to time. He was friendly with the kids from Johnny's Restaurant. They listened to the jukebox music, got drunk on cheap wine, hung around Second Street, or went for rides when some of them were old enough to have cars. One of them, "Tutti" Migliori, would panhandle for money on the street. When he got fifty cents, he would buy a pint of "Sneaky Pete" wine and chugalug it. If he got enough money, he would chugalug two or three bottles in a row until he stumbled and became incoherent.

Ray Letkowski wasn't as bad as that. Although he drank a lot, a predilection he inherited from his alcoholic dad, he was bright, especially in math and logic. After high school, his parents sent him to Villanova University. He graduated with a BS degree and later married a good woman with whom he had several children. As he got older, he stopped drinking. That decision—and the good woman—probably saved his life, although he died of a massive heart attack when he was close to seventy. That's not a bad age, considering his track record.

I also liked Ray Perez. Ray was a good pool shooter and made money Saturday mornings playing nineball at Kelly's. He was born in America, though his parents had emigrated from Coruña, Spain. He worked in a machine shop as a patternmaker and made good money, compared with the rest of us. He was good-looking and dated regularly, but didn't want to marry and settle down. He had several steady girlfriends with whom he would get together to get laid. He never wanted the relationships to go beyond that. I liked and admired him and would try to pick his brain about how he managed to get laid so often, but he never went into detail.

I often thought about getting married. In retrospect, it might have helped me to mature, but I was conflicted about women. My ideal images of women were either Hollywood starlets or nice Lithuanian girls. I didn't know any Hollywood starlets and the Lithuanian girls I knew, for the most part, didn't really like me. They aspired to marry someone with a future, something I didn't seem to have. I can't say that I blamed them. If I had been in their shoes, I wouldn't have looked at me as an exciting prospect, either.

One Lithuanian girl to whom I was attracted thought I was a dork. Our parents were social friends and our mothers made an effort to get us together. Her mother strongly suspected her daughter of messing around with guys and wanted to hook her daughter up with a "good boy" like me. But, like me, this girl had self-worth issues. She was sexually active and already having affairs with some of the good-looking Lithuanian guys. She blew me off. I knew one of the guys she had dated and he told me, point-blank, that he had banged her. While guys usually exaggerated their sexual exploits, it was apparently true in this case. She missed at least one of her periods, I found out. To my knowledge, she did not give birth to a child, though. Since abortion was still illegal in that era, it's possible that the fetus aborted spontaneously.

Another Lithuanian girl to whom I was attracted seemed to like me. She was only eighteen and had recently emigrated with her family from Lithuania. I'm not sure how they were able to get out of Lithuania at the time, since it was still occupied and governed by the Russian Communists. They must have bribed somebody to get out.

At any rate, my hormonal attraction to her was very strong. She was young and pretty. We sat on the grass on summer nights, petting heavily, but she was quite practical and wanted a man to marry. She brought me home to meet her parents. Her father, who spoke very little English, had a janitor's job here in the United States, although he was educated and had been a forester in Lithuania. He asked me a series of questions in order to see, I guess, if I was a good enough prospect for his daughter. "How much education do you have?" he asked.

"I graduated from high school and am taking some night courses at Rutgers in Newark."

"What kind of work do you do?"

"Well, I work with a house-siding contractor now, although I see myself moving on pretty soon."

"What do you plan to move on to?"

"Well, I'm not sure about my prospects right now, but I plan to finish college in the future."

Those answers didn't go over too well with the father and that ended the affair with his daughter. Shortly thereafter, she married someone more acceptable to him.

Some of the local American girls liked me, but I didn't like them—at least not enough to marry them. One young woman from a nice Italian family made a real effort to attract me. We dated several times and she even gave me a gift of leather gloves for Christmas. Even though she was a cut above the girls on Second Street, I wasn't attracted to her. She wanted to marry and settle down; I didn't—at least not with her.

I was attracted to other American girls whom I felt were more thoughtful and more genteel, but they weren't attracted to me. They probably correctly sensed that I had some sort of idealized image of them rather than seeing them for the real people they were. I dated only because I was lonesome, not because I wanted to develop a meaningful relationship. To be honest, I wasn't sure what a meaningful relationship was.

CHAPTER 15
THE LAST STRAW

At some point during this period of drifting, I began to doubt that I would reach my dream of "making it" in America. As much as I disliked the thought of accepting my lot, I began to think that maybe I should cease the struggle, accept reality, and settle down to the blue collar/lunch bucket world around me. I decided to try some of the blue-collar jobs that were available. For once, I wouldn't have to come up short in terms of the educational requirements as I did when seeking white-collar jobs.

At Dad's urging, I applied for and got a job on the assembly line at the General Motors plant in Linden, New Jersey. The pay was relatively good and it made Dad happy because I was the second son to follow in his footsteps. (Ray was also working there at the time.) Dad didn't believe I would succeed in getting a college degree, or that I could get (and keep) a white-collar job, so my working at General Motors made sense to him.

Ray worked in the paint shop. My foreman took me to see him the first day I was there. I guess it was his way of easing me into the General

Motors family. The paint shop was filled with a mist from the paint being sprayed on the bodies of the cars. Most workers wore masks, although Ray didn't. He also smoked on breaks and after work. For a person who'd had tuberculosis as a youngster, this was rather remarkable—but not inconsistent with his bravado attitude.

I was given a job on the second floor of the factory, at the end of the body assembly line. That's where the assembled bodies were transferred onto a conveyor belt that carried them to the motor assembly line one floor below. My main duty was to make sure the assembled bodies being transferred to the conveyor belt stayed separated properly. As they transferred to the conveyor belt, a felt-padded separator with an electronic sensor would be raised by a hydraulic motor to keep the three or four bodies apart from each other. Occasionally the sensor would malfunction and the hydraulic motor wouldn't raise the felt-padded separator. That's where I was supposed to jump in and keep the bodies from banging into each other.

Since the sensors didn't malfunction very often, I was lulled into a sense of complacency. I focused, instead, on one other duty I had, which was to glue rubber hoses onto the bodies where the front fenders were to be attached. It was a rain seal, as I remember. At any rate, I would feed the hoses through a mechanical glue roller and then attach them to the two front chassis parts. Since this task was a routine no-brainer, I would do five or ten in a row, working my way up the assembly line. That would give me some free moments to work on the *New York Times* crossword puzzle I kept at my workstation.

I bought the paper every day to read during my breaks, or to work on the puzzle when I could. After I'd worked my way up the line, I'd get absorbed in the puzzle until the line moved the cars to where I had finished gluing the rubber hoses. I would then start gluing the hoses up the line again. I paid little attention to the conveyor belt.

That was my downfall. One of the sensors on the conveyor belt malfunctioned one fine day and two bodies started to bang into each other. This started a chain reaction that prevented any bodies from going down to meet the chassis. Caught completely off guard, I panicked and pulled the emergency chord that stopped both assembly lines. That idled three or four thousand employees and, in effect, shut down the entire production part of the factory. Since they were all union employees making fifteen or twenty dollars an hour, the cost to General Motors with each second of lost productivity mounted exponentially.

The foreman, normally a very nice and patient man, ran up to me up screaming at the top of his lungs. "Mankus! What the hell are you doing?!"

He pushed the banging bodies apart on the moving conveyor belt, re-engaged the sensor, and hit the restart button that got the two lines moving again. He came up to me where I stood helplessly by my workstation and saw the partially completed crossword puzzle.

"What is this?" he asked.

I didn't know what to say. He chastised me for being inattentive and repeated the instructions for dealing with a sensor malfunction. He didn't fire me or assign me to a less responsible job, even though I made the same mistake on one other occasion. I was the second generation of my family to work at the plant and the third member of my family on the payroll, so that must've carried some weight. Either that or I wasn't any worse at the job than the guy who had had it before me.

But I couldn't take it anymore. I pretty much hit bottom at that point. I realized that if I continued to work there I'd probably go crazy. Literally.

I knew in the depth of my being that I was capable of much more. I knew I'd never be happy unless I reached higher and did what I had to do to get there. As difficult as it was for me, I had to face the fact that higher education was not just the preferred path, but the *only* path to survival.

I began to understand, more or less, that I had a new mission now: I would have to rewire my brain. My brain had been wired early on for survival as a refugee in the chaos of war, for the post-war existence in a refugee camp, and for the hardscrabble life of poverty in a new land. I began to realize that those skills would not help me to progress beyond survival in America. The rules of progress in America were different, more abstract. I began to realize that I'd have to muster what skills I had to adapt to the more genteel world of academics, social interaction, and other things to which I had yet to be exposed. I had an inkling, though, that they had to do with mental and emotional discipline, as well as postponement of gratification.

At any rate, I decided to go after that college degree, no matter what. I had been taking evening classes, on and off, at Rutgers in Newark. Now I decided that I would enroll on a full-time basis as soon as I could, and hang in there until I graduated. While school was a mental and emotional challenge, I decided that it couldn't be any worse than working on the assembly line of General Motors, or bartending at Lithuanian Liberty Hall. If I went crazy in school, I said to myself, it wouldn't be any worse than going insane on the assembly line at General Motors.

I'm sure I could've enrolled at Rutgers in Newark, but I wanted a clean break and a fresh start. A fresh start would give me new motivation, I thought. While that logic was questionable, I clung to it. Alex, one of my Lithuanian DP acquaintances, had graduated from Fairleigh Dickinson University. It was a tenuous connection, but I decided to apply there. Even though Alex wasn't a close friend, I was hoping that his success would rub off on me somehow, or at least give me the stamina to survive the long and lonely nights when I had to read assignments and write reports.

As an added incentive, I decided to major in English. It was another perverse way to motivate myself. My logic was as follows: the only course I had ever flunked was the English class in my junior year in high school. Ms. Murphy (God rest her soul), didn't think I had much potential. Although I wasn't a star student by any stretch of the imagination, I usually passed my courses with respectable Bs and Cs. I wanted to prove to Ms. Murphy, and to myself, that I could do it.

In addition to my perverse logic, I also had dreams of becoming a writer one day. Mr. Benjamin, another English teacher at Thomas Jefferson High School, had seen a glimmer of hope for me. One day he read aloud to the class an excerpt from one of my essays. He used it as an example of good writing. It surprised me because I had just whipped it off as part of a quiz he gave us. But that encouragement lit a little light of hope in me. Writing was one of the few things for which I seemed to have a talent. At least it didn't require math.

There was also a lot of political and social energy in the air in that era. It was 1965 and the Vietnam War was going full blast. The Baby Boomers had come of age and were starting to protest on college campuses across the country, especially since the draft was still in effect. The Civil Rights movement had started to ferment and blacks were protesting in the South and in large urban centers in the North. The Kinsey Report and *Playboy* magazine contributed to the sexual revolution.

Those were heady times of change in America. Although I wasn't personally involved in any of the movements or protests, I was keenly aware of what was going on and gained motivation from the energy of all that turmoil. I wanted a piece of the action and saw college as a possible way to get it.

Ironically, one of the few "successful" ventures I was involved in during this period was a bowling league. Somebody at Kelly's came up with the idea of starting a bowling league. I was OK with that. I always liked games and there were enough of us to start a league of about six or eight teams. Those of us with the highest bowling averages got together as would-be team captains and took turns choosing our teams. It was a draft of sorts.

One of the would-be team captains couldn't come to the meeting because he had to work, so we picked his players for him. We tried to be fair about it. While we didn't go out of our way to stack the best players in his favor, we usually gave him the player with the next-highest average when his turn to pick came around.

That didn't work out too well. When he found out the next day which players had been picked for him, he protested vigorously and complained that we had shafted him. He went on at length, whining about his team, which he claimed was the least competitive in the league.

After listening to his complaints for a while, I decided I couldn't take it any longer. I don't know if my reaction was based on an honest sense of fair play, bravado of the moment, or just some sort of skewed logic, but I grandly offered to exchange his players for mine. If nothing else, I just wanted to shut him up.

He jumped at the chance and agreed instantly. Kelly authorized the switch and the league was off to a start. I didn't think it would make much difference. We all felt sure that the team captained by a guy named Mike would take first place. Mike was tall and athletic. He bowled in several other leagues every week and had an average in the high 180s. He was by far the best player in the league and we felt sure that his team would run away with first place.

But to everyone's surprise, Mike struggled with his average and his team languished in second place. My team of "rejects" jumped into first place and continued to distance itself from the rest of the teams as the season went on. Not only that, but I had the highest average in the league at 171. Mike was second, trailing me by several points.

There was some sort of chemistry between the "rejects" and me. They felt proud, apparently, to be on my team and we cheered each other on. They felt grateful, I guess, that I had picked them and they didn't want to let me down. They all bowled way above their previous averages.

Just when it looked certain that we would run away with first place, fate—or reality—stepped in. I had just gotten a job on the night shift at the General Motors assembly plant and couldn't continue to bowl. I apologized to the team and asked them to go on without me. They could use my average every game, minus ten pins, which was the league rule. We were so far ahead near the end of the season that there was a good chance that the team could coast to victory with just a few more wins.

But the team couldn't win without me. They lost game after game. By the last match of the season, they needed to win two of the three remaining games to stay in first place. I made the decision to call in sick to my boss at General Motors and join my teammates for the last match against Mike's second-place team.

It was a tough decision to make. First, I had just started at General Motors and knew that my boss wouldn't be too happy about my taking the night off. He didn't buy my lame excuse of feeling sick. Second, the team had lost the momentum we'd had before I abandoned them and there was a good chance it was too late to recapture it.

The players were a little down that night. They felt dispirited and perhaps betrayed by my abandoning them to work at General Motors. We lost the first game, and needed to win the next two to finish the season on top. I called the team into a huddle. I tried to think of what a coach would say in the locker room to a football team at halftime.

"Look guys, I'm sorry I abandoned you halfway through the season. It was my fault. Don't blame yourselves for my mistake."

I looked briefly at them. Their eyes were lowered, but they were listening.

"But we had something before I left, didn't we? I don't know what it was, but we had it."

A few mumbles of agreement.

"Mike's team was supposed to run away with first place, but it didn't happen. Why didn't it happened?" I paused and looked at them again. They were quiet. They didn't know what to say.

"Us! That's what happened," I said firmly.

A few nods. A couple of "yeahs!"

"They had us written off. We were the underdogs."

A few more "yeahs!" This time, they were a little stronger.

"And you know what? We decided we'd play as a team. That's what we had. We had teamwork."

"Yeah!"

I invited them to reach out and stack our hands.

"*Teamwork!*" we chanted and broke off to bowl.

Little by little, we began to regain the old chemistry; we started to bowl with the spirit and enthusiasm of the past. We managed to eke out a win in the second game and continued on to win the third. We were champions of the league by one game.

It was never the same after that. Mike quit the league because he didn't like the lanes and the league broke up after only one year. We couldn't get enough players to field at least six teams, but the memory of that year gave me lift.

.

CHAPTER 16

FAIRLEIGH DICKINSON UNIVERSITY

The summer of 1965, I started to attend classes at FDU with renewed energy for academics. The job experiences of the past few years had kick-started my motivation; the stick of the real world was more persuasive than the carrot of my dreams had been.

I started with evening classes. I didn't have enough money to attend school on a full-time basis yet. I wasn't aware at that point that student loans were available. Even if I had been, I'm not sure that I would've qualified. Also, I wasn't too keen about getting into debt. I didn't think of tuition as a good investment in the future yet, what with my shaky academic track record.

So I quit the job on the assembly line where I had worked the evening shift and got a day job with another house-siding subcontractor. I didn't earn much, but at least I was able to attend classes in the evening.

I didn't have a car, so I commuted by public transportation. It was an hour and a half one way from Elizabeth to Fairleigh Dickinson's Rutherford campus and another hour and a half back; two buses each way. I chewed Maalox tablets to relieve the acid burn in my stomach from the boredom and ennui.

While the newfound motivation helped me to do better academically, I wasn't satisfied. I wanted what I thought was a "true college experience." My image of that came from watching college football and basketball games on TV many a Saturday afternoon at Kelly's. I was impressed by how the students came out in droves to cheer for their teams. I wanted to be part of the hoopla surrounding the games—the marching bands, the pretty cheerleaders, the team mascots, the crazy costumes and painted faces of the students, the large signs, and the hype of the TV announcers and commentators.

I'd also seen pictures in newspapers of college students cramming themselves into a phone booth, or into a VW Beetle, to break previous records and I wanted to experience that crazy, carefree world. While one side of me saw these antics as inane and silly, the other side, the one that wanted to belong, observed that there was a tolerance—an admiration almost—for such foolishness and I wanted to be part of it.

After one semester of commuting, I applied for a student loan and got one, although it was barely enough to cover tuition; room and board wasn't included. So I mooched off my parents and any other relatives I could buttonhole. With Mom, I cashed in the chips. A few dollars at a time, she paid out the shoeshine money I had given to her years before, although I don't think she fell for my efforts to put her on a guilt trip about it. She realized as well as I did that she had given me much more than I ever gave to her.

I also hit up my brother, Henry. He was an adult by now and had been drafted into the Army. He was deployed in Vietnam, where he served as a medic. I wrote letters to him regularly, asking for money. He always came through; maybe a hundred bucks at a time. I kept careful track of what he loaned me in a little book and repaid him everything, years later, after I started to work.

I wish I could say that I repaid him gladly. It wasn't that I wanted to cheat him out of the money. My reluctance was due to the fact that he was never the same after he came back from Vietnam. He saw combat there. One of the incidents he described was riding in an ambulance that ran over a land mine. The explosion killed the soldier next to him. Henry wasn't hurt, but he was shaken badly.

After he was discharged, he started drinking and smoking pot, probably a continuation of a habit he'd picked up in Vietnam. He hooked up with a woman from Newark who was about twenty years his senior. She provided him with food and shelter, as well as pot and booze. He couldn't seem to hold a job at that point and was always in need of money. He kept after me to pay him back what he'd loaned to me.

At first, I paid him back in dribs and drabs, along with lectures about getting his act together. But it didn't take long for me to realize that my lectures had no impact. He liked to hear them because they gave him an opportunity to play along with me and tell me—as well as himself—that he was on the verge of getting it all together.

It didn't really bother me that he thought he was fooling me; what bothered me was that he was fooling himself. I could see that he had the drug addict/alcoholic's gift of self-deception and that there was nothing I could do about it. He had to do it himself. I finally got frustrated and paid the balance of my debt in a lump sum.

It was sad. He had completed most of his college credits before he was drafted. He needed to take only one or two more courses to get his BS degree in chemistry from Rutgers University. He never did. He never went back to school, even though he could've taken advantage of the GI Bill.

During his high school and college days, he had a beautiful young girlfriend. She cared deeply for him even after he came back from Vietnam, but she, too, finally gave up on him. She had to go on with her own life and couldn't continue to nurture someone who couldn't take care of himself. He drifted from job to job and eventually qualified for medical disability payments from the Army. He was diagnosed with bi-polar disorder, among other things. No one talked about post-traumatic stress syndrome in those days; I'm not sure that the medical community had gotten much beyond the World War II concepts of "shell shock" or the euphemistic "soldier's heart."

I thought about the day Henry came home from the hospital after he was born. I remembered looking at him in Aunt Eva's arms and seeing him contort his lips as if to say something. Maybe it wasn't an involuntary contortion, I thought now; maybe he had been trying to tell me something about his future. I also remembered how he almost fell out of the train when we were leaving Lithuania and how guilty I felt that I didn't wake everyone to warn them of the danger. Raudys had saved him, of course, but now I felt guilty again. Was I supposed to be my brother's keeper? Could I be my brother's keeper? I didn't know how to be one. If he didn't want to help himself, there was nothing I could do. But I still felt badly.

He would call from time to time, usually after he had been drinking. He would talk nonstop in a euphoric voice, telling me how he was getting his act together; saying that he was on the verge of turning his life around. I'd try to steer the conversation to his actual situation. Where was he living? What was he doing for money? How was his health? But it was hard to have a meaningful conversation with him; I pretty much just listened to his monologue. After a while, I would say good-bye to him, feeling empty and sad.

One time my brother, John, and I had some reason to go to New Jersey together. John lived in California at the time and I was living in Chicago. I talked John into stopping in Elizabeth to see Henry. I was hoping that our visit would motivate Henry somehow; give him some hope, maybe.

Henry lived in a small flat on the third floor of a building on Orchard Street. It's hard to say what kind of a building it had been originally, but at the time, the owner operated a tavern on the first floor and rented out small apartments on the two floors above. Henry had one room that served as a bedroom and a living room and a small kitchenette.

Henry and the landlord were buddies. Henry worked in the tavern on a part-time basis and took us down to meet him. Henry told us that he trusted the landlord and gave him any money he'd save up for safe-keeping. That sounded a little strange to us, but we didn't want to interfere with any relationships Henry had built up. We stayed for a little while and chatted with Henry and the landlord, but the conversation dried up before long. We couldn't think of much to talk about and we said our good-byes.

At one point, Henry dried up and stayed that way for about five years. I'm not sure if our visit had anything to do with it, but I was happy to hear it. As always, I hoped that he would turn his life around. Even though he was well past middle age, it's never too late, I felt.

I was still living in Chicago when he called one day. "Henry! I'm glad to hear from you," I said. "How are you doing?"

"I'm good; how about you?"

"We're all good."

"Good. I'm glad to hear that. I just called to say hello."

"Are you still on the wagon?"

"Yeah, I'm taking my bipolar meds, but I'm not drinking."

"I'm so proud of you, Henry. Keep it up."

He sounded normal. But shortly thereafter, he received a lump sum settlement of $61,000 from a car accident he'd been involved in, and that changed everything. He suddenly acquired many new "friends" who wanted to hang out with him and help him spend some of that cash. He began to celebrate this windfall and the combination of the bipolar medication and alcohol was his undoing. The bar owner called the police after Henry failed to respond to his loud knocking. The police forced open the door to his apartment and found his body. He had been dead for about three days. He had been eating pizza and watching TV when he just keeled over and died on his bed, several months short of his sixtieth birthday. The pizza slices were still there. He died alone, except for the two cats that lived with him. I still have the pictures Henry sent to me of him with the cats.

Those of us siblings who could make it flew in to New Jersey and buried him. Ray, who lived in the Jersey shore, arranged a Mass for him at Saints Peter and Paul Church in Elizabeth and we said our final good-byes.

But that happened many years after Henry loaned money to me to pay my way through Fairleigh Dickinson. Besides Mom and Henry, I hit up Great Aunt Diode. She didn't have much beyond her monthly Social Security check.

I always liked her—loved her, really, although I'm not sure I would've called it that at the time. She was always praying for me, especially when I started to attend FDU. She'd see me studying in my room, hour after hour. I would come out every once in a while and pace the floor in the hallway, trying to motivate myself. Since her room was next to mine, she'd see my frustration, and she'd pray for me. I'd see her praying with that infinite patience she had and I'd go back to my room and study some more.

She was my surrogate mom, I guess, and I felt badly about the way the family took her for granted. At times I thought Mom and Dad treated her unfairly. She was always expected to do the lowly and menial household jobs no one else wanted to take on. So I wanted to help her in any way I could. Sometime after I started school, I found out that she might be eligible for Social Security benefits. Even though she had never worked outside of the family unit or paid any money into the Social Security fund, there was some sort of provision that allowed people over seventy to draw modest benefits. I managed to secure a one-hundred-dollar per month stipend for her.

Diode was happy and proud to get this money. It was the first time in her life she'd had an income. She was grateful to me and promised to redouble her prayers for me. I'm sure she did. The money gave her a sense of self-worth that she'd never had before. After she suffered a pulmonary edema and was unable to get around much, she'd ask Father Juozas Pragulbickas, the elderly Lithuanian priest from Saints Peter and

Paul Church, to visit her once a month to pray with her. It gave her great satisfaction to be able to give him a five- or ten-dollar donation. From time to time, when I was desperate for funds, I would ask her and she'd give me a few dollars.

That lasted for several years, until she, too, died. She never recovered fully from the pulmonary edema and deteriorated rapidly thereafter. We buried her in a local cemetery. I didn't cry at the funeral but I've never forgotten her. To this day I pray for her soul from time to time.

So, anyway, going to school full-time wasn't the college experience I had imagined it would be. Beside the money problems, I could never get over the feeling that I was an outsider. Part of it had to do with the fact that I was older than most of the students (I was already twenty-six when I started at FDU), but the main sense of alienation came from inside me rather than from the other students.

The first full-time semester, I lived by myself in an apartment off campus. Then I met another student who offered to share his place with me. He had dropped out of a small, elite, liberal arts college in the Midwest and transferred to Fairleigh Dickinson, which was near his home. His family lived in a large house in Rutherford, just a few miles from the main FDU campus. It seemed funny to me that they'd pay for him to live on campus when their home was so close. But they appeared to be wealthy, so money wasn't an issue, I guess.

He was younger than I was, but older than most of the other day students, which, he thought, gave us something in common. He made an effort to befriend me, inviting me for dinner at his parents' home and asking some of his attractive female friends to come visit us from time to time. But I did not feel comfortable with him, with his family, or with his friends; I wasn't confident enough in myself to reach out to people whose background was so different from mine.

But in spite of my insecurities and sense of alienation, a few good things did happen. First and foremost, I was continuing to stay in school and earn college credits. That's more than I had been able to accomplish in the past. It was a challenge, though. Some of the courses, like Eighteenth-century English Literature, for example, drove me nuts. Writing analytical essays about foreign authors who had died two hundred years ago seemed absurdly abstract. But I plugged away. I checked the dictionary for every obscure English word that I ran across and noted its meaning in the margins of the book.

I did enjoy some courses, especially if the professor made an effort to get the students involved. One political history professor wouldn't allow us to sit passively while he lectured. He threw thought-provoking questions at us, making us think.

Good professors seemed to motivate me—even in subjects like math. I got an A in one math course I took at FDU. It was taught by a professor who was also a dean. He was low-key and unassuming. He had a step-by-step approach and explained things verbally, rather than numerically, which made the concepts more clear to me. At one point, he assigned a problem that I solved in a way that was different from the way shown in the answer book. I got the same answer as the one in the book, but the professor scratched his head over my methodology.

Prior to my senior year, I applied for and was accepted to the Honors Program. Chancellor Peter Sammartino started the program to guide and assist exceptional students to achieve their academic goals, including any independent study they might choose. I was pleasantly surprised to be selected because my grades weren't great. Maybe it was the essay I wrote about my immigrant background. Chancellor Sammartino, the son of poor Italian immigrants who came to the United States through Ellis Island, probably related to that.

Dr. Sammartino retired shortly after starting the program. He lived on for another twenty-five years, but shot his wife, Sally, and then himself in a murder/suicide in 1992. He was eighty-seven years old and his wife was eighty-eight. They'd been married for more than fifty years. They never had any children—other than the students at FDU. They had been in failing health. Sally had Alzheimer's disease and Peter had undergone surgery to remove a kidney. No note was found but the police recovered a 38-caliber revolver. Sally had been shot in the temple and Peter was shot in the mouth. Maybe it was a love pact to end their lives together.

At any rate, I was grateful to be selected for the Honors Program. I think it was the first time in America that someone had seen a glimmer of potential in me and backed it up with a tangible reward. I received a five hundred scholarship and other privileges, such as assignment to a personal mentor.

My first mentor was Dr. Charles Angoff. He was in the English Department at FDU and had written some books, mostly dealing with Jewish immigrant themes, as I recollect. He was familiar with Lithuania, which had had a large Jewish population for hundreds of years. Leonard Saunders, the director of the Honors Program, thought he might be a good fit for me—a role model, maybe.

It didn't work out that way. Dr. Angoff was a nice man, but I didn't feel a strong kinship with him. Though our backgrounds were similar in some respects, they were essentially different. The deeply tragic story of the European and Russian Jews was not my story. Dr. Angoff made a list of books for me to read, including classics like *The Buddenbrooks,* by

Thomas Mann. He added some of his own books to the list, but I didn't like them. In all fairness, though, few books were enjoyable or relevant to me at the time. I was too busy with my regular schoolwork and too wrapped up with my personal challenges to enjoy extracurricular reading. The only exceptions were books on outer space, the universe, or the subatomic realm. Those were, and still are, fascinating topics to me. I would've considered majoring in any of those fields except for the fact that they all required good math skills.

In the next (and last) semester at FDU, I asked Mr. Saunders to assign Professor Algirdas Landsbergis, who taught European history, to be my mentor. He was a Lithuanian immigrant and a well-known writer in the Lithuanian community. He had written extensively both in Lithuanian and English, including poetry, plays, short stories, and a novel. I liked him better than Dr. Angoff. He was very patient and didn't try to impose any particular agenda on me. Like me, he had experienced cultural alienation, although his wasn't as bad as mine was, I thought. He was twenty-five and fully steeped in Lithuanian culture when he came to the United States, so he didn't seem to have the identity issues that I had. In addition, his education had provided him with a worldview that was broader than mine was. He began his studies in Lithuania at the Vytautas Magnus University in Kaunas, and went on to study at the Johannes Gutenberg University in Mainz, Germany, after the second Russian occupation in 1944. After he and his family immigrated to the United States, he got a master's degree at Columbia University in New York.

The thirty students in the Honors Program held regular weekly meetings. Either Mr. Saunders or we students selected topics for those meetings and invited speakers to present them. The topics were wide-ranging and included politics, computers, poetry, biological clocks, etc. I invited Professor Landsbergis to one of the meeting and he spoke about the theater of the absurd.

I enjoyed those meetings with the other members of the Honors Program, some of whom were older, like me. I felt comfortable and intellectually stimulated in that kind of forum and participated freely. One of the speakers discussed hypnotism and actually hypnotized several students during the meeting, instructing one of them to do well on a test he had to take in his next class. He was awakened from the trance and told to go take the exam. I never found out how he did, but he was a good student so I'm sure he did OK.

I also was chosen for a study-abroad program in Cuernavaca, Mexico. It was in the summer of 1967, between my junior and senior years. I received another student loan for the trip. Sally Sammartino, who was the dean of admissions and director of the study-abroad program, helped me with the paperwork.

It turned out to be a great experience. We were there for six weeks. We stayed at the beautiful home of Dr. and Mrs. Nelson. Dr. Nelson was the retired dean of libraries at FDU and had acquired this property in an elegant section of Cuernavaca, called Privada Las Quintas. The Nelsons and their staff organized trips for us to archeological sites, museums, and villages with silver artisans. We were usually accompanied by people steeped in the relevant topics.

One trip was to the Cathedral of Cuernavaca, an elegant church built some hundreds of years ago by the Spanish monks who had converted the indigenous peoples to Catholicism. The new bishop, Bishop Arceo, had stripped the walls of the church to their original finish and instituted a popular service on Sundays called the *Misa Panamericana*. The American tourists who became familiar with it began to call it the

"Mariachi Mass," because local Mariachi musicians performed liturgical music written and composed by Mexicans and sung in Spanish.

One of Bishop Arceo's ideas was to make the church and the mass reflect the people and the culture of Mexico. Another was to draw more men into church. What better way, he thought, than having Mariachi musicians wearing their masculine charro outfits play romantic violin and stirring trumpet music in church?

He was right. The men turned out in droves, followed by even more women, children, and tourists. It was a huge success and an affirmation of Mexican culture.

I decided to write the required course paper on the Mariachi Mass. I read the available literature on it and interviewed the lead soloist. Marilú Robertson, the Nelsons' adopted daughter, helped me in the project. She was a Mexican girl, about sixteen at the time, although she was mature for her age. She took a liking to me for some reason and followed me around wherever we went with the group. I took advantage of her bilingual skills and asked her to serve as my translator and icebreaker whenever I needed to speak to the locals, including the lead soloist of the mariachi musicians.

I got an A on the paper. (*See the Appendix for "The Mariachi Mass in the Cathedral of Cuernavaca."*) That paper and that trip started what turned out to be a long-term relationship with Latin America.

I graduated from FDU with a bachelor of arts degree in June 1968. I felt relieved because I had finally achieved at least one major goal I had set out for myself, a goal that put me on a path with some possibility of advancement. It was my first tangible step toward integration into the American middle class; toward a sense of belonging.

CHAPTER 17
PEACE CORPS

The six weeks I spent in Cuernavaca, Mexico, reinforced my decision to minor in Spanish and join the Peace Corps after I graduated from FDU. I'd been thinking about it for several years, partly because I liked President Kennedy. He and his wife were young, attractive, and energetic. America, like most of the world, had fallen in love with them. His assassination in Dallas less than three years after he took office froze him as an icon of idealistic possibilities, even among some political conservatives. The Peace Corps was one of his legacies. He'd started it as a way to reach out to less economically developed countries with young volunteers from America.

Mom and Dad weren't too happy about that decision. The Peace Corps paid its volunteers just enough to live on. Dad thought I was chasing idealistic rainbows and not facing up to the responsibility of making a living. He didn't see an upside to the sacrifice.

As a practical matter, he was right. But I still hoped there was more to life than just economics. "Ask not what your country can do for you.

Ask what you can do for your country," President Kennedy said in his inaugural speech on January 20, 1961. My three brothers had done their part for our new country through military service. I couldn't do that because I'd been classified 4-F, ineligible for military service, when I was called up for a physical exam by the Selective Service System, otherwise known as the Draft Board. That happened in 1961, right after a diplomatic incident that became known as the Berlin Crisis—the second one since World War II.

After I received the letter to report for the initial physical exam, I felt, at least momentarily, as if the traumatic events of World War II were coming back to haunt me. I thought we'd left them behind when the war ended and we moved to the United States. But the decisions made by President Roosevelt at the Yalta Conference in February 1945 had geo-political consequences that lasted for half a century thereafter. In exchange for several concessions, including Stalin's promise to join the Western Allies militarily against Japan, Roosevelt agreed to hold back the Western Allied troops and let Russian armies take the Eastern and Central European countries in the final drive to defeat Nazi Germany. Despite warnings by Churchill and William C. Bullitt Jr., US ambassador to the Soviet Union, Roosevelt said, "I just have a hunch that Stalin is not that kind of a man…and I think that if I give him everything I possibly can and ask for nothing from him in return, noblesse oblige, he won't try to annex anything and will work with me for a world of democracy and peace."

I'd never heard anyone use the words "noblesse oblige" and "Stalin" in the same sentence before. It's possible that Roosevelt's assessment of Stalin was clouded, in part, at least, by his poor health at the time.

Roosevelt died of a massive cerebral hemorrhage on April 12, 1945, several months after the Yalta conference. He was sixty-three.

Stalin's noblesse oblige led him to tighten his grip on the countries he occupied with Soviet troops and never hold the free elections he'd agreed to at the conference. He also began to chomp at the bit regarding his section of Berlin, which had been partitioned between the four powers. In 1948, he demanded that all Western convoys, which carried food and other provisions to West Berlin, be searched. Even though the Western Allies had free access to their zones in Berlin per the Potsdam Agreement of July 1945, Stalin figured that he had the upper hand because they had to pass through Soviet-controlled territory.

When the Western Allies rejected Stalin's ultimatum, he blocked all surface traffic to Berlin. That started what became known as the First Berlin Crisis. The start of the second crisis—the one for which I was called up by the draft board—began in October 1961, although the events leading up to it had started much earlier. Between July 17 and August 2, 1945, the four allies met in Potsdam, Germany, to decide, among other things, the fate of Germany following its defeat. They decided to divide Germany and Berlin into four sectors to be governed by the four allied countries. Their long-term goal was to govern Germany jointly until the country could be reunited into one political entity.

Once the cold war started, though, the Eastern and Western Sectors diverged politically. The model for the West German sector was a Western democracy and it prospered economically with the aid of the Western Allies through the Marshall Plan. East Germany, organized as a Communist country with centralized control a la the Soviet Union model, lagged further behind West Germany with each passing year. The result of this economic disparity was the migration of millions of

Germans, including many students and professionals, from the east sector to the west sector.

Looking for a way to stop the flow of people from east to west, Nikita Khrushchev, the wily protégé of and successor to Joseph Stalin, declared that it was time for the United States and the Western Allies to pull out. President Dwight Eisenhower and, later, President John F. Kennedy, rejected that ultimatum. Attempts to settle the dispute diplomatically weren't successful. In fact, tensions escalated after East Germany erected the Berlin Wall. President Kennedy responded by increasing the Army's strength from 875,000 to approximately 1 million men and ordered draft calls to be doubled.

I reported for the physical exam with my buddy, Mack (Vyto Maceikonis), who'd also gotten the notice. That's when I found out I had no eardrum in my right ear. Apparently it had deteriorated from all the ear infections I'd had in my youth and they classified me as 4-F, not acceptable for military service. Mack passed the physical with flying colors and was sent to Germany, where he served for two years. He also met and married a German woman there.

So after I graduated from FDU in June 1968, I thought I'd serve my country by joining the Peace Corps. I was accepted for a two-year assignment in Ecuador, subject to my passing a ten-week training course that summer. The letter stated that I had to report to Montana State University in Bozeman immediately after graduation. It included a blank airline ticket that had to be filled in at the ticket counter.

I was happy that I'd been assigned to a Spanish-speaking country. I was good at languages (a lot better than at math, anyway) and was already starting to understand and speak Spanish from the courses I had taken at FDU and from my trip to Cuernavaca.

I went to the Newark airport with my one suitcase and presented the ticket to the pretty reservation clerk. "I want to fly to Bozeman, Montana," I said.

"Where?" she asked, her lips forming into a smile. Her tone of voice was playful, a cross between mock incredulity and mild sarcasm.

"Bozeman, Montana," I repeated, playing along with her.

"Wow!" she exclaimed. "It sounds like a swinging place."

It was flattered that a pretty girl behind the counter had dropped her professional cool and seemed to be taking a personal interest in me, but I wasn't really up for the light banter. After all, I was joining the Peace Corps. That was a big deal. When my smile faded, she resumed her professional demeanor.

"Will that be a round trip, sir?" she asked.

"No. One-way."

Her eyebrow arched slightly, but she held back from asking me the obvious: what the hell was I doing flying to Bozeman, Montana, and not coming back? Finally, I volunteered the answer.

"I just joined the Peace Corps," I said, "and I'm flying to Bozeman for training."

"Oh," she said, somewhat placated. She seemed curiously interested in what I was doing. I think she was hitting on me. That was a new experience for me. Maybe I should've asked for her phone number.

At any rate, I joined a group of sixty or seventy other volunteers at the campus of Montana State University. We were an eclectic group, a mixture of recent college graduates and some older types. Most were single, though some were married, including a recent law school graduate and his wife. A number of the young men in the group had joined to avoid the draft. Some made no bones about it and admitted as much, although a number of the franker ones were culled by the administrative staff before we were sent to Ecuador.

During the ten-week program, we received language training and basic information about the country, including its geography, history, culture, and customs. We learned that Ecuador is located on the western coast of South America, the side facing the Pacific Ocean, between Colombia to the north and Peru to the east and south—right around where the geographic equator crosses the continent. That's probably how it got its name. It also straddles the Andes Mountains, the backbone of the continent. Climatically, though, Ecuador is divided into three distinct regions: the warm coastal region; the moderate *altiplano* of the mountains; and the tropical *Oriente*, on the eastern side of the Andes, which tapers off into the rain forest of the Amazon Basin.

We also learned that Ecuador is an independent country of about fourteen million inhabitants within an area of approximately 100,000 square miles. It was colonized in 1561 by Spanish conquistadores led by Francisco Pizarro, who conquered the native Indians of the Inca Empire. In 1968, the Ecuadoran government was ostensibly democratic, although many of its freely elected rulers had been overthrown by military juntas since it gained its independence from Spain in 1822.

The training staff included native speakers, some from Ecuador, who drilled us in Spanish. We started out with daily lessons of three or four hours, but increased rapidly to seven or eight. The emphasis was always on speaking, never on reading or passive listening. One of the favorite drills of the lead instructor was to gather us in a circle, put us into an imaginary setting, such as a restaurant, and bark rapid questions at us, compelling us to respond quickly with orders for food or drinks. We had to shout our answers back in Spanish; the quicker the better. He didn't care if we made mistakes as long as there were fewer of them as we progressed.

That method was effective, I thought. After ten weeks, many of us had a Foreign Service Institute (FSI) rating of two or greater, which meant that we could converse comfortably in casual settings. I felt confident after ten weeks that I could get along on my own once I got to Ecuador.

Finally, we were given a general orientation about living in an economically less developed environment. That last part may have been an eye-opener to some of the volunteers who hadn't been out of the country before, but it wasn't a big stretch for me. In order to see if we had the mettle to survive in that type of environment, we were tested on what they considered to be survival/self-reliance skills. They sent us out into the surrounding area for a couple of days with only a few dollars in our pockets. They wanted to see if we could manage to find a place to sleep, get some food, and get back safely to the MSU campus by a designated time.

I found my way to a ranch where I was hired to help load bales of hay onto a truck. In exchange, I was paid twenty-five cents an hour and fed. By coincidence, I also got a chance to observe a forest fire up close. I didn't have to do much since the ranchers and the local firefighters brought in a lot of heavy equipment, but that experience made a lasting impression on me. I wrote a short article on my three-day adventure and it was published in "Ecuador 518," the typewritten and mimeographed publication of the volunteer trainees in Bozeman. (*See the Appendix for "Big Sky Country."*)

To my surprise, the article was well received. Most of the other volunteers wrote articles or poetry critiquing the training program or the Vietnam War. Those volunteers were the liberal, activist types, many from Eastern colleges. They comprised about half of our group. The others were more traditional volunteers who wanted to do good for the disadvantaged. They were irritated by the activists, who politicized the training process and Peace Corps, in general.

I didn't have a draft problem so I was able to focus on the training experience itself. When my article about the three-day survival trip came out, the traditional volunteers were especially complimentary, though some of the activists seemed to like it, too. I was happy about that. I didn't want to be caught up in the ideological squabble between the two groups.

By the end of the ten-week program, a number of the volunteers had been cut and others had quit—"self-deselected" was the euphemistic term for that. They had decided that draft or no draft, the Peace Corps and/or Ecuador wasn't for them. They may have found other ways to avoid the draft, especially if they were lucky enough to have higher lottery numbers. The remaining thirty or forty of us were flown to Quito, the capital of Ecuador.

At its center, Quito is about 9,350 feet above sea level. It took us a few days to get acclimated to this altitude, but we were mostly young and healthy and it wasn't a big deal. It's not even as high as La Paz, the capitol of Bolivia, which rises to over 11,000 feet above sea level. After additional orientation and some administrative paperwork, we were sent out to our various sites around the country. Within a week, I was sent to Santa Rosa with Roger Dellwo, another volunteer from our group.

Santa Rosa is a small town in the province of El Oro in the southwestern part of Ecuador, not too far from the Pacific Ocean. Its climate is warm, bordering on tropical. At the time, it had a population of about 20,000, consisting mostly of small merchants, farmers who had small plots of land in the countryside, and the poor who worked for them. Many of the farmers cultivated bananas, the main crop of Ecuador. My job was to work with Arcelio Ordoñez, the manager of a credit coop.

Arcelio was a good manager and had a handle on the operation. He didn't really need my help. Arcelio suggested I get involved with the banana farmers in the area to help them form and run a banana cooperative. That seemed like a doable goal and my motivation rose. I helped them to get things off the ground by holding several meetings. As I remember, we formed the coop and had it registered with the proper authorities. We also elected officers and held some strategy sessions.

They seemed to appreciate what I was doing, but I didn't see that we were making any progress on the big issues, like selling the bananas to wholesalers when there was an oversupply of the crop and a rock bottom price for it. That's when I realized that my contribution would be marginal, at best.

Roger, my fellow volunteer, was an honest-to-goodness farmer from Minnesota and helped the local farmers raise pigs. He was a hands-on volunteer and didn't mind getting into the mud of the farms and the muck of pigpens. My motivation and skills in that area were zero. Unlike Roger and some of the other "technical" volunteers, I was a "generalist" with no practical skills.

A few of the generalist volunteers did get deeply involved with the locals and seemed to provide meaningful help, at least on a small scale. Joe Romance, one of the volunteers from our group, was a good example. He hooked up with Lucho Molina and his family in a village called Boca de los Sapos. (Literally translated, it means "mouth of the toads.") He helped them to start a corn demonstration plot, dig new wells, diversify crops, budget their money, raise chickens, improve their pig stables, and market their crops. In turn, they treated Joe like their own son.

But I didn't have a very giving personality. Helping the small banana growers around Santa Rosa was the extent of my accomplishment in Santa Rosa. I questioned my usefulness to Ecuador and to Peace Corps in general and started to think about leaving.

I wasn't alone in that regard. Many of the volunteers, even the technical ones, such as teachers, engineers, and farmers, felt ambiguous about their roles. They felt they were simply being used as free labor rather than changing or improving the systems in which they were involved.

Some of the generalists, however, worked directly with the native Indian population, the Quechuas, who were among the most disenfranchised. I called these volunteers, like Bob Henderson, the "purists." They lived among the native Indians and tried to "raise their consciousness" by simply being with them and/or getting drunk with them occasionally on *chicha,* a homemade brew of corn fermented, in part, through bacteria from saliva.

Sometimes these volunteers helped the native Indians to resettle in the Oriente, the eastern part of Ecuador, which was still sparsely settled and where land was still cheap. The Oriente, at the edge of the rain forest, had a largely tropical climate. The roads and infrastructure were rudimentary or nonexistent, somewhat akin to America's "Wild West" before it became settled—except it was hotter, more humid, overgrown with flora, and overpopulated with fauna.

After a while, even the purists realized that they could help a few families here or there, but it was beyond their power to change the entrenched socio-political and socio-economic order of things. Ecuador had three distinct classes of inhabitants: the whites, the *mestizos,* and the Indians. The rich of the ruling class were descendants of the white, Spanish colonialists, also known as *criollos*. They were large landowners and industrialists. They comprised about 15 percent of the population and generally married among themselves and/or immigrants from European countries. They retained the political and financial power in the country.

The *mestizos*, the largest demographic group, comprised about 55 percent of the population. They were mostly the descendants of the Spanish colonizers who had intermarried with the native Indians. They represented the middle or lower middle class of merchants and educated or semi-educated majority of Ecuadorans. The family of Lucho Molina with whom Joe Montana worked, for example, were *mestizo*.

The native Indians, descendants of the Incas, comprised about 25 percent of the population. They didn't intermarry outside of their own ethnicity and remained the working poor who scraped a living off the land. They, along with a small group of Afro-Ecuadorans living in Esmeraldas and Imbabura provinces, were largely disenfranchised, politically and socially. They had little, if any, education; some didn't even speak Spanish, the *lingua franca* of Ecuador.

I wasn't idealistic enough to do what the purists did and not trained to be of use in some small, practical way, like Roger Dellwo was. For nine months, I made a valiant effort to be useful and to get involved with the local population as best as I could, but it didn't work out. Mostly I was bored and lonesome. I read a lot and tried to hook up with some local girls.

Roger Dellwo and I shared a small apartment on the second floor above a drug store in the center of the town. We had a faucet in the kitchen and running water usually, but when we turned it on, the water was rust-colored. Occasionally, small lizards would come out of the tap with the water. Of course, we boiled the water before drinking it, but the pot we boiled it in would turn black from the dirt. We took malaria tablets every day.

It was hot and humid most of the time and we had no air conditioning. We kept the windows open to catch what little breeze there was. But the street noise was a tradeoff. The jukebox in the bar nearby played music full volume until four in the morning and then started up again several hours later when customers started to arrive. The owner of the bar was particularly fond of Julio Jaramillo, an Ecuadoran singer with a beautiful tenor voice. He was by far the most famous singer from Ecuador. He recorded many songs, the most famous of which was a sad ballad that was very popular at the time, called "Nuestro Juramento." The owner played it over and over again for the customers, or the would-be customers who hung around the small plaza in the center of the town until all hours of the morning. Most of them were unemployed, bored, and lonely—like me. Some of the younger men were suspicious of us volunteers. They believed that we worked for the CIA and were there to further America's imperialistic goals.

Many of the younger women liked us, though. They saw us single guys as rich Americans and potential husbands who would take them away from their humdrum existence to an exciting future in America. In my case, that was a joke, of course. But I was flattered. Even some married women showed interest in us. The wife of the druggist who owned our building would find excuses to come and visit me in the apartment from time to time, sometimes in the morning while I was shaving. She was fascinated by how much shaving cream I used on my beard, she said. She was still fairly young and attractive, and I was tempted to taste the forbidden fruit, but I played it cool. I was concerned about compromising the Peace Corps in some way.

The women's interest in us was probably part of the reason the young men were resentful of us. But a few of them reached out and befriended me. Maybe they liked me. More likely, they saw in me a possible opportunity to better their lot in some way. I didn't make any effort to mislead them, but I did enjoy their attention and friendship. That's about all I had going for me.

Herman, also single, was a little younger than me. He was my liaison of sorts with the local community. He introduced me to some girls and showed me the ropes, so to speak. There were the evening *paseos* when all the single girls and young men would come out for an evening stroll around the main plaza to see and be seen—somewhat akin to "cruising" in the United States, except without cars. We cruised several times and made a few contacts.

He also showed me the rundown barrio with the row of little cabins where the cheap prostitutes worked the johns, mostly the enlisted men from a nearby military base, though some of the locals patronized them as well. It was done on an assembly-line basis. Every five minutes or so, the girls would spill out a basin of water in front of their cabin and come out for the next john.

Sex was an open reality in Santa Rosa, as it was in all of Ecuador generally. There were the "good girls" and the "bad girls." The good girls were either attractive and/or came from a family with financial resources. They were marriage material and didn't engage in pre-marital sex, though they did turn on the honey charm when they wanted to attract a man. The bad girls, on the other hand, were unattractive and/or so poor that they had to earn a living any way they could. Some married women played around as well—if they found someone they liked. In bigger cities, like Quito or Guayaquil, for example, some of the more attractive married women supplemented their income by working in the classier houses of prostitution.

Ecuador was about 90 percent Roman Catholic at the time. While the Catholic Church was officially opposed to sexual licentiousness, as a practical matter it was an accepted reality of life. Everyone understood that, even the young teenage girls.

I befriended some of the nicer girls, even had crushes on some of them. There was Maria Elena, for example. She was only sixteen and very pretty. She had won a local beauty contest. She seemed to like me and I was enchanted by her. I was twenty-nine years old already and you'd think that I would've known better. Her father watched me like a hawk to make sure there was no hanky-panky. Nothing came of our flirtation, but it was painfully sweet while it lasted.

After nine months, I couldn't take it anymore. I packed my things and left for Quito where I intended to turn in my resignation to the Director. I suppose I could've lasted the remaining fifteen months to complete the two-year assignment, but I decided to be honest with myself and with Peace Corps. I didn't want to admit that I had failed, but it was better to go back to the United States than to continue to live what, in reality, was a charade.

Travel in Ecuador was an adventure. To get to Quito, you first had to take the bus to Guayaquil, the largest city in the country. There were no buses directly from Santa Rosa to Quito. In the coastal towns many of the buses, especially the local ones, had wooden bodies and no glass in the windows, because of the warmth and the lack of air conditioning. During carnival time, before Easter, the lack of glass lends itself to mischief. Everyone is in a festive mood and there is a social acceptance of naughty merriment. One of the customs at the time was to fill balloons with water and throw them at the passing busses. This was harmless, although sometimes the water balloons also included flour.

From Guayaquil, you transferred to another bus, a diesel Mercedes Benz usually, and took the eight-hour trip up the mountains to Quito. That ride, through the narrow, winding roads with hairpin turns along the sides of the Andes Mountains, in the dead of night, was dangerous. The drivers clipped along much faster than we volunteers considered safe.

The reverse journey down the mountains from Quito to Guayaquil was even more hair-raising. Gravity gave the bus greater speed and from the right-hand lane, passengers could look hundreds of feet down the steep-sided canyons along the way. Encountering an oncoming car, truck, or another bus on the narrow, two-lane road prompted a less-than-elegant dance to see which driver would give way to the other. Counter intuitively, the night trip was safer since the driver could see headlights from around the bend before the oncoming vehicle was in front of him. That gave him time to slow down and pull over.

I remember one trip in particular from the coast to Quito. A group of us had traveled to the coast from Quito to participate in some of the carnival fun for the weekend. Right after we arrived, I contracted a either a stomach virus or food poisoning. I vomited repeatedly until nothing was left in my stomach. Even then, the nausea didn't go away.

I decided to leave the group and take the bus back up to Quito to seek medical help with our doctor at the American Embassy. I left my friends and took the first bus heading toward Guayaquil. Since this was a no-window bus, I was repeatedly doused with water balloons. Nobody seemed to notice that I wasn't in good shape. Maybe all of us gringos looked alike.

After I got to Guayaquil, I transferred to a large, Mercedes Benz diesel bus with windows. I didn't get doused with water, but then I had to endure the hairpin turns of the mountain road to Quito. Fortunately, my stomach was totally empty by then and I just dry-heaved.

The bus made stops periodically for gas and bathroom breaks. I was pretty much dehydrated by then and didn't need any bathroom breaks. The young street vendors would board the bus and try to sell us fried snacks. I'd often bought them on previous trips, but I passed that time.

When I finally got to the American Embassy in Quito, I found out that the doctor was away for the weekend. There was a nurse on duty along with a skeleton crew of marines. She gave me her home recipe to fight nausea: Coke with sugar. The sugar killed the carbonation (which might have induced more gagging) and the coca in the Coke seemed to alleviate the nausea. I felt better almost immediately. I wished I had known about that home remedy before I took the twelve-hour trip to get back up the mountain.

I met with the director, Joe Haratani, in Quito and informed him of my decision to terminate my assignment. I told him that I didn't feel very useful. Joe, a very nice man of Japanese/American descent, asked me to stay on and accompany him on his visits to various volunteer sites in Ecuador.

The offer surprised me. After giving it some thought, I agreed. I accompanied him to a few sites, but again, I felt like a visiting dignitary with no real duties. Some of the volunteers and paid staff resented my special, seemingly baseless privileges. Shortly thereafter, Haratani asked me to make independent visits to towns that had requested Peace Corps volunteers. He wanted me to help evaluate the feasibility of placing future volunteers there.

I liked this second offer better than the first one and tackled it with some enthusiasm. It gave me the opportunity to see the country, talk to the locals, and write about my observations. I visited a number of locations and wrote reports about them for the director. He seemed to enjoy reading them. Some of the positive reports I wrote ended up in the hands of future volunteers, who read them before locating to the site. Some of the negative reports never made it beyond the director. I was particularly proud of my report on the town of Muisne. I couldn't honestly recommend that the Peace Corps place a volunteer there, but the town was beautiful in a tragically sad sort of way. (*See the Appendix for "Muisne."*)

During this period of about nine months, I got to know Ecuador a little better. I also began to realize that my skills were in observing, analyzing, and reporting, not participating in the trenches. I devoted the last six months of my two-year assignment in Ecuador to preparing and publishing a bilingual magazine called *El Ecuador*. The previous editor and staff had left at the behest of the new director because their focus had been more on what was going on in the United States than on the realities of Ecuador. I tried to change that. I solicited articles, drawings, and photos from the volunteers and put them together into the one and only issue we managed to publish.

The Christmas before I finished my tour in Ecuador, I took some time off for a vacation and traveled to Peru, where I visited all the touristy spots: Lima, Cuzco, and the Inca ruins of Machu Picchu. Something happened on that trip that left a deep impression on me; something that encapsulated my Peace Corps experience.

I had just been to see the Inca ruins above Cuzco, the ones called Sagsayhuaman, and was coming down the dirt road when I came across a herd of llamas. There were eight or ten of them. They walked slowly, sniffing the air before them, or snipping a few blades of grass now and then from the side of the road.

They had long necks, small heads, and rabbit-like noses. They bobbed and weaved, now lowering those small heads to feed on the grass, now raising them to sniff the air. One of them, probably the leader, stared at me for what seemed like a long time and then, as if he'd lost all interest in me, walked over to the side of the road for a mouthful of grass.

They all wore striped saddlebags and I was curious to find out what was in them. I noticed an Indian resting on the side of the road, so I tried to strike up a conversation with him.

"What do the llamas have in those bags?" I asked him in Spanish.

"Llama dung," he said.

I shouldn't have laughed, but I did. I glanced at another tourist standing there in the middle of the road. He was smiling and taking pictures of the llamas. I don't think he knew what was in the bags either.

"Where are they going?" I asked turning to the Indian again.

"Do you see those two over there?" he said, pointing behind the herd.

I followed with my eyes to where his finger pointed and saw an Indian woman and a little boy, perhaps seven or eight years old, coming up behind the herd. The woman carried a baby bundled on her back and supported herself with a stick. The little boy walked quickly alongside, carrying what looked like a two-gallon tin can.

"Yes," I said. "What about them?"

"Well, they are taking the herd back to their village high in the mountains. They live near the snow, where wild horses run, and where even trees don't grow. Every once in a while, her man loads up the llama herd with dried dung and sends it with his wife and two children down below here to the town of Cuzco."

"It must be a long journey," I said.

"Yes. The journey begins early in the morning, long before the sun has risen, and doesn't end until she gets back to her village, after it is already dark."

Now it wasn't so funny.

"Where does she take the dung?" I asked.

"She takes it to the *chichería* here in Cuzco. The *chichería* feeds it to the fire that burns under the big *chicha* vat. You know what *chicha* is, don't you?"

"Yes," I answered. "It's what you drink. It's what makes you feel good."

The Indian nodded and smiled.

I looked at the tourist again. He was still standing there in the middle of the road snapping away with his camera. He was in the way of the llamas, so they turned off to an even smaller and steeper path and continued walking. The woman and the little boy followed them.

"How much does the woman get for the dung?" I asked the Indian.

"The *chichería* pays her six *soles* for each saddlebag."

I crunched the numbers in my head. That's about fifteen cents a bag, I realized. With the eight or ten llamas in the herd, she made a dollar and a half. After fifteen hours of walking up and down a mountain, she made a lousy dollar and a half.

"What does she do with the money?"

"She buys *chicha*," he said. "See the tin can in the boy's hand? It's filled with *chicha*."

I looked at the tourist again. He was rewinding the roll of film in his camera. He looked satisfied. I guess he was thinking about the great shots he had gotten for the folks back home.

CHAPTER 18
IRS-NEWARK

My assignment in Ecuador ended in August 1970. After a two-year hiatus trying to live idealistically, I came down to earth and "reality." It wasn't pretty. The US economy was in a recession and I couldn't get a job. My hopes for some sort of a Foreign Service assignment with the US State Department or the Agency for International Development (AID) didn't materialize. I did come close to getting into AID, though. The agency was looking for advisors and/or foreign aid administrators in the northern part of South Vietnam. It was at the height of the Vietnam War and American soldiers, government officials, and agents of Non-Governmental Organizations (NGOs) were being killed—not to mention civilians. Against my better judgment, I was willing to consider it as a way of eventually getting into the Foreign Service. Fortunately for me, AID rejected me, possibly because of my nonexistent eardrum.

I went back home to Elizabeth, New Jersey. I had nowhere else to go. They say home is the one place they can't turn you away. I'm not sure that's always true, but my parents didn't turn me away. They simply accepted my return the way they accepted everything else they couldn't change. They had no idea what I had gone through in the past two years and they weren't interested. My Peace Corps experience had had no impact on their lives in any way; their lives revolved around their home, their jobs, and, above all, around the economic reality of survival. They were interested in my helping them with the household expenses, not in listening to stories about Ecuador. They had never been in favor of my joining the Peace Corps.

So I stayed home and mooched. I watched TV, ate lots of ice cream, and gained weight. It felt as though my two years of sacrifice had meant nothing. It hurt Mom to see me mope and feel sorry for myself, so she took the initiative to talk to a neighbor of ours, a wealthy old gentleman for whom she did household work from time to time. He was well connected in the area and agreed to talk to the director of the Union County Welfare Department about hiring me.

That worked. I got a job as an assistant to the fraud investigator who chased after welfare cheats, such as mothers who claimed to be single while they were sharing their homes—at least some of the time—with their husbands or boyfriends. It wasn't a fun job, but it paid a modest salary.

About this time, the federal government was actively seeking revenue officers for the Collection Division of the IRS. I received the announcement in response to my application for the more glamorous Foreign Service assignments. They must've passed it on to the IRS.

My first reaction was to throw it in the wastebasket. I couldn't see myself working for the IRS. I didn't like numbers, accounting, or taxes. But I hesitated. Even at the height of my idealism, I maintained a modicum of common sense. Having worked on the assembly line at General

Motors and tended bar at a neighborhood tavern, I thought twice about turning down a potential opportunity. I put the announcement away to think about it. Compared with the welfare department, the IRS looked good; the pay would certainly be better. The starting salary was close to thirty thousand dollars per year—pretty good money in those days.

So I filled out the application and sent it in. It was to be my fallback position in case something better didn't turn up. When I was summoned for an interview, I went in with long hair and an attitude. I didn't really care if I got the job or not. Ironically, that's probably what got me hired.

Frank Del Mauro, a man in late middle age who later became my group manager, interviewed me. After asking me a few warm-up questions to put me at ease, he threw me a slider. "How would you justify your desire to *give* to people," he wanted to know, "with the need on this job to *take* from them?"

The question surprised me. I'd never thought of myself as a giving person, at least not in the missionary sense that he seemed to mean it. Having grown up poor, I was always trying to get things, not give them away. But he was probably typecasting me because of my Peace Corps experience.

"I don't have to justify anything," I responded sharply. "Don't impute personality traits to me due to my Peace Corps experience."

It wasn't an illogical question, of course. If I hadn't known any better, I might've assumed the same thing. But I did know better. I knew that half the volunteers in my group had joined the Peace Corps to avoid the draft.

He must've liked my answer. He probably thought I had spunk. That's a quality you *do* need when trying to collect money for the government.

When I received the offer of employment some weeks later, I decided to accept it. I had no better prospects and was unhappy at the County Welfare Department. My manager there was a small-town blowhard who didn't like me. He was a former drill sergeant type with a big girth and a crew cut who probably saw me as a liberal "pinko," unfit for the job of catching welfare cheats. The only reason he put up with me was that I'd been hired on the recommendation of our influential neighbor. As narrow-minded as he was, he had enough political savvy to know that you don't mess with references of influential people. Of course, I didn't tell him that this influential neighbor could not have cared less if I'd been fired.

I started work for the IRS at its Newark office in September 1971. I was placed in a group of sixteen trainees who had been hired about the same time. The plan was to keep us together for the one-year training period, managed by Frank and his assistant, Russ D'Arcangelo, a GS-11 revenue officer selected by Frank to be his trainee coach.

We were a diverse group: young college graduates, middle-aged men, some women, and a few miscellaneous types (for lack of a better term), like me. Diversity was a strong suit of the federal government at the time, although it was not always by design. Originally, the low pay and dull work contributed to this diversity. More qualified candidates didn't want to work for the government; they usually got more glamorous and better paying jobs in private industry. Later, when the government pay scale was increased to compete with private industry, the IRS started to get applications from more qualified candidates and diversity and political correctness became more deliberate hiring goals.

The young college graduate group included Mike and Steve. Mike was a third-generation Polish/American who was in a state of denial, I thought. Like me, he didn't want the job. He took it because he thought it would keep him out of the army. He declared himself a conscientious objector. He wasn't a vocal protester in the sense of actually demonstrating against the Vietnam War, nor was he ready to leave the country and go to Canada as a number of young men did at the time, but he didn't want to fight in a war that he didn't believe in. I can't say I blamed him for that, but I didn't buy his pacifist line either.

Steve had pale skin and long hair that kept falling over his eyes. His clothes were disheveled and rarely blended into a harmonious ensemble. His shoes were scuffed and misshapen and the tip of his belt was never quite tucked into the loop at the waist of his trousers; it sagged over like the neck of a dead goose. He was nonassertive and quiet, but during breaks he liked hanging out with the young, college graduates, with whom he became more relaxed and animated. I thought he fit the pacifist role better than Mike.

The middle-aged men's group consisted of Bernie and Juan. Bernie was in his early forties, married, with a grown son. He had been through a number of jobs in his life, never staying very long in any of them. I didn't expect him to stay very long in this one, either. I didn't think his heart was in it. (Whose was? The standard joke among us was that tax collectors belonged to the second-oldest profession in the world.) Bernie had graduated from law school and was obviously qualified for the job— overqualified, I'd say, except for the fact that he was never able to pass the bar exam. After trying four or five times, he finally gave up. He had a self-deprecating sense of humor about that, though it often cut too close to the bone to be really funny. It surprised me to find out, about five years later, that he was still there. Maybe he just gave up trying to find something he really liked. Like me, I'm not sure he knew what he really wanted to do.

Juan was a retired army veteran, a non-commissioned officer (NCO), who took the job to supplement his military pension. He was given a hiring preference because he was a vet, including a five-point boost on the exam we took when we applied for the job. He was very correct and straitlaced. He rarely joked around and never spoke Spanish with me even though I tried to entice him into it from time to time. He wanted to be more American than the Americans, something he'd probably learned in order to survive in the Army. I couldn't help but think, though, that, like me, he was a man of two cultures who was not fully integrated into either one.

The miscellaneous group included Dave, Harry, and me. We were all about thirty years old with some work experience. Dave was a quiet, intelligent engineer who lost his job when his company downsized, forcing him to go outside of his college training and personal comfort zone to be a collection officer with IRS. He was an unassuming bachelor who accepted this unfortunate turn of fate with equanimity and a self-deprecating sense of humor. I liked Dave and got along well with him, although I had more ambition for succeeding at the IRS job than he did.

Harry had transferred to the IRS from the Post Office, also with a score preference because of his government service, but he could never quite get the hang of being a revenue officer. He got hung up on the "trees" of the procedural minutiae and never saw the "forest" of banging heads to collect money for the government. His efforts to make it were as comical as they were pathetic and he was let go before the end of the one-year training period. I think he went back to carrying a mailbag at the Post Office.

I wasn't a woman, a military veteran, or a minority. (I guess they didn't consider immigrants to be a minority or disadvantaged in some way.) But I was a *college graduate*. After falling short in the past, it felt good to finally measure up to the qualifications for a white-collar job.

The first year was largely a training period with lots of classroom instruction. Periodically, we'd get some "hands-on" experience, though that was mostly watching and observing full-fledged revenue officers doing their jobs. Typically, we accompanied the revenue officers when they went out to seize assets of a tax delinquent. The managers considered seizures to be the highest and "sexiest" calling of the job. From time to time, they would let us go out on our own and make contact with taxpayers, usually on simpler cases, like those requiring us to pick up delinquent tax returns.

I found the training to be a piece of cake and was eager to become a full-fledged revenue officer. I thought I could handle the job independently without any difficulty. Also, I was getting tired of what I thought were the ego trips of Russ, the trainee coach, who wanted to "break me in." Among other things, he made me do menial jobs, like making photocopies. I think he and Frank, the manager, saw me as a little too independent.

After the first year, I became a full-fledged Grade 7 revenue officer. The pay was about thirty thousand dollars per year, which I considered to be terrific money. I started to pay off my school loans, bought a new car, and took care of some medical issues. Frank Del Mauro asked us to indicate our preference for a post of duty in the Newark District. I didn't care to which office I was assigned, I told him, except that I wouldn't like Jersey City. It was a rough, blue-collar town, not much different from Elizabeth, in some respects, except that the monstrous Pulaski Skyway gashed diagonally through the middle of it. It seemed like a stretch of pavement for people on their way to New York City.

So, naturally, Frank Del Mauro assigned me to Jersey City. Maybe it was his way of getting even with me for not living up to his initial expectations for me. One of my first experiences there lived up to *my* low expectations for the town. I was driving slowly near the center of town when an old woman in dirty clothes suddenly darted into the street, right in front of my car. I jammed on the brakes and tooted the horn in anger. The old hag let out a stream of expletives and spat on my windshield.

Welcome to Jersey City, I thought.

I was stationed there for about two years, working routine small cases, chasing after delinquent taxpayers. If an individual or a business didn't pay, we had the power and authority to take administrative enforcement action without the need to seek court permission. We could levy on their bank accounts, garnish wages, and/or seize property, such as cars, homes, machinery, and equipment. We also had the power to shut down businesses by putting locks on their doors, although that power was greatly diminished after the 1977 US Supreme Court decision in *G.M. Leasing v. United States, 429 U.S. 338.*

My motivation was fairly good during this period. The job was a lot better and more interesting than most of the ones I'd had in the past. I was learning new things, including a legal perspective. It was the kind of learning I enjoyed. Unlike high school or college, which was all reading and theory in sterile classroom settings, this was on-the-job learning with a practical connection to what I was doing. In addition, I was being paid to learn. How can you beat that? My manager, Mr. Olin, was fairly nice and gave me good reviews. I'm sure he was aware of my shortcomings, but I think he recognized that I had some potential. He made me feel better about myself.

After a while, though, the job became routine. My scope was still narrow and limited, I thought. I longed to expand into a bigger arena. I applied for other positions within the IRS, trying to work my way up the career ladder. One of the jobs I applied for was a Grade 9 revenue officer's position at the Office of International Operations (OIO) in Washington, DC. It meant more pay and overseas travel. While I didn't get the AID or Foreign Service positions I had hoped for, this sounded close—or at least as close as I was likely to get.

CHAPTER 19
IRS-OIO

I moved to Washington, DC, with a lot of optimism and anticipation. I was finally getting away from home, had enough income to support myself, and it looked as though the job would be interesting enough to make a career of. But even if it wasn't, I loved the idea of travel. It was crazy: we could travel virtually anywhere in the civilized, non-Communist world. We took trips to Europe, Canada, Latin America, and the Far East.

My first official trip was to Guam, which has been a US territory in the Pacific Ocean since the Spanish-American War of 1898. It's a small island, not too far from the Philippines. It's only about thirty miles long and, depending on where you are, only four to twelve miles wide. It had a population of about 150,000 at the time. The weather there is hot and humid with little temperature variation throughout the year. It's located in what has been nicknamed "Typhoon Alley" due to the likelihood of tropical storms and typhoons during the wet season. I was there during one such storm, but it was only a category 1 or 2 and didn't cause much damage.

I stayed there for sixty-eight days collecting unpaid Social Security taxes. While Guam has a local government, including a governor and a legislature, as well as local income taxes, the residents are subject to the US Social Security Act, which means that the employers and their employees have to pay FICA taxes. Much like in the mainland US, some employers withheld the tax from their employees' wages but failed to turn it over to IRS, along with the employers' matching share. So we had to go out there and collect it from them—by enforcement action, if necessary.

The enforcement action could be anything from bank levies to seizures of the businesses. One employer, a large warehouse, was particularly recalcitrant and I had to shut it down. I walked in there on a Friday morning with several assistants, including a fellow revenue officer who was on the trip with me, and an IRS auditor. In addition, I got the help of a local locksmith and several local police officers, who came along at our request.

The employees were intimidated by this show of force, but didn't know what to do. The owner wasn't there, so they continued to work with their heads down, as if nothing had happened. I took out my official government ID and raised it above my head.

"These premises are under seizure by the United States government for nonpayment of taxes," I announced firmly. "Please pick up your personal belongings and vacate the premises at once."

The employees did as they were told and I ordered the locksmith to install padlocks on all the doors. This secured the premises and prevented anyone from entering without my authorization. Incidentally, it also made the US government legally responsible for any theft or damage that might occur. For that reason, it was important to inventory of all the items in the warehouse. We didn't want the owner to make any false claims against the government.

Frank Del Mauro, my former manager in Newark, might have been pleasantly surprised by my lack of hesitation to "take." I saw it simply as something I had to do. It was my job. It was certainly legal, although it could be unpleasant at the human level. My experience with previous seizures, though, was that most taxpayers responded obediently to a seizure and submitted peacefully to the indignity, as they did in this case.

That was not always the case, though. Taxpayers sometimes resorted to counter-intimidation, or even violence. On September 23, 1983, for example, taxpayer James F. Bradley, who was then sixty-three, shot and killed revenue officer Michael Dillon in the kitchen of Bradley's home. Bradley, a former employee of the IRS, was audited by the IRS six months after he left the service. The IRS determined that he owed an additional $2,500 for the 1981 tax year. Bradley had paid the IRS $2,000 over a period of time. Dillon was attempting to collect the remaining $500.

Bradley told Dillon that he couldn't cover a check for the $500 and that Dillon would have to wait until Bradley received his next Social Security check. Dillon insisted on immediate payment, however, and asked Bradley for consent to seize his belongings. Upset, Bradley left the kitchen and returned bearing an M-1 rifle. He ignored his wife's pleas to put the rifle away and walked within three feet of Dillon, who was seated. Bradley aimed the rifle at Dillon's torso, and said, "Mike, are you prepared to meet your maker?" He shot Dillon once, then shot him again as Dillon attempted to stand. Dillon fell to the floor. Bradley kneeled down and felt Dillon's pulse. He then shot Dillon again.

Revenue Officer Dillon didn't use good judgment in that case and paid with his life. It was unfortunate for everyone involved, including Bradley, who was convicted of manslaughter and incarcerated.

In another case, one in which I was personally involved after I left IRS, I represented a fifty-six-year-old businessman from Cleveland, Ohio. Before he contacted us to represent him, he told me that IRS had seized his belongings from his home. He said two IRS revenue officers, accompanied by their manager and several armed special agents, knocked on the door of his home about seven thirty in the morning. When he answered, the revenue officer in charge of the case showed him a writ of entry issued by the US District Court and demanded entry. He was taken aback and became disoriented, he said, but didn't offer resistance.

Once the IRS agents were inside, though, he became an unwilling actor in a surreal play. The IRS agents informed him that they were there to seize his property. They began to inventory the furniture and other items that they considered to be potentially valuable and called in the movers, who were waiting in a van parked by the house. Upon orders of the lead revenue officer, the movers started to carry out the furniture and other personal property.

The taxpayer's wife then came out of the bedroom and became upset when she realized what was going on. She started to cry and retreated to the bedroom in an effort to compose herself. Wanting to comfort her, the husband followed. But if they thought they would get a moment of privacy in their own home, they were mistaken. The armed special agents followed them into the bedroom. Under the circumstances, they were concerned that the taxpayer, or even his wife, might have a weapon in the bedroom and would come out shooting.

The IRS's powers have since been circumscribed by the Internal Revenue Service Restructuring and Reform Act of 1998, which President Clinton signed into law on July 22, 1998. In addition, in the landmark decision by the US Supreme Court in *G.M. Leasing v. United States*, 429 U.S. 338 (1977), the court had held that an entry without a warrant onto the private areas of personal or business premises of a taxpayer for the purpose of seizing property to satisfy a tax liability is in violation of the Fourth Amendment to the Constitution. This decision effectively stopped IRS' long-standing practice of seizing the assets of a business regardless of whether they were located in public or private areas, and simply padlocking the premises.

My seizure of the warehouse in Guam took place before those changes took effect. I secured a set of keys from the locksmith and locked all the doors. There were too many items in the warehouse to be inventoried that day. In addition, much of the property in the warehouse belonged to other businesses and wasn't subject to our seizure. It had to be segregated from the property belonging to the employer and turned over to the rightful owners. That was a logistical and time-consuming can of worms.

I decided to come back and inventory all the personal property at a later date. If need be, I would go through the tedious process and then schedule a public auction within thirty days if the employer failed to pay the taxes due. I was hoping to avoid it, though. From past experience I had learned that, confronted by the shock of an IRS seizure, some taxpayers become desperate and scramble with a variety of eleven-fifty-nine-before-midnight ploys, including bargaining, begging, and calling their accountants, lawyers and/or bankers, in an effort to stop or delay the proceedings. Some even manage, at the last minute, to come up with the money due.

That's what happened in this case. The owner's attorney called the following Monday and came in with a cashier's check to fully pay the taxes due, including interest and penalties. That solved my problem of having to do a very tedious inventory.

Our seizure of the warehouse was big news on the island. It hit the front page of the local newspaper. One reason was that the publisher had a huge roll of paper stored in the warehouse and had called to find out when and if he would be able to get it out. By way of explanation, I provided him with enough information for next morning's front-page story. The lien we had previously filed against the taxpayer had made the tax liability a public record already and I didn't have to worry about an improper disclosure.

My trip to Guam was either a first for IRS collection, or one of the first. It was certainly the first time that the IRS had executed a seizure on the island to enforce collection. There was some concern among the Washington managers that the locals would react negatively to this show of force. In fact, the locals were respectful of our authority. The managers in Washington, DC, seemed relieved and pleased with the way it turned out.

We IRS employees worked out of the offices of the local tax authority in Guam. The director of that office, as well as his assistant, were retired Americans who had previously worked for tax agencies in the US. Even though we and the top staff of the local tax authority were *Haoles*, the Hawaiian term used by the locals to describe white non-locals, there seemed to be no real resentment local employees. We became friends with many of them and interacted socially, including dating. I dated Cece, a woman about my age. She was exotically beautiful to me in a Eurasian sort of way. I never asked about her bloodlines, but she seemed to be a mixture of Asian and Filipino, and perhaps native Chamorran.

I did some research later to learn more about Guam. Based on archeological artifacts found on the island, one theory is that the original settlers were seafarers from southeastern Indonesia who inhabited the island about four thousand years ago. Over the centuries, they developed into their indigenous ethnicity and culture, which they named Chamorro.

The first Western person to reach Guam was the Portuguese navigator Ferdinand Magellan. Sailing for the king of Spain, he reached the island in 1521 during his fleet's circumnavigation of the globe. General Miguel López de Legazpi claimed Guam for Spain in 1565. Spanish colonization of Guam began in 1668 with the arrival of Padre San Vitores, who established the first Catholic mission.

Guam and the other islands in the Mariana chain were part of the Spanish East Indies governed from the Philippines, which were, in turn, part of the Viceroyalty of New Spain based in Mexico City. Between 1668 and 1815, Guam was an important resting stop for the Spanish Manila galleons, a fleet that covered the Pacific trade route between Acapulco and Manila. While Guam's Chamorro culture is unique, the cultures of both Guam and the Northern Marianas were heavily influenced by Spanish culture and traditions during their 333 years of rule.

The United States took control of the island after the 1898 Spanish-American War as part of the Treaty of Paris. Guam came to serve as a station for American ships traveling to and from the Philippines, while the Northern Mariana Islands passed to Germany, and then to Japan.

During World War II, Japan attacked Guam on December 8, 1941, one day after the infamous attack on Pearl Harbor. The resulting Japanese occupation lasted approximately thirty-one months. During this period, the indigenous people of Guam were subjected to forced labor, family separation, incarceration, execution, concentration camps, and forced prostitution. Approximately one thousand people died during the occupation.

The United States returned on July 21, 1944, and recaptured the island as well as the rest of the Northern Marianas in the Battle of Guam. Congress passed the Guam Organic Act in 1950 and established Guam as an unincorporated organized territory of the United States. Among other things, it provided for the structure of the island's civilian government and granted its inhabitants US citizenship.

So it's possible that Cece had a mixture of genes from the indigenous Chamorro and one or more of groups that had occupied Guam over the previous centuries. She spoke very good English and worked for Guam's attorney general, another retired American transplant. We'd go out to various social functions and/or play cards with her family and friends during inclement weather.

My stay in Guam was enjoyable. Besides the fact that the job and the social life were going well, my living accommodations and nutrition were well beyond what I had been used to in my youth. I stayed at the Okura, a very fine Japanese hotel, and enjoyed gourmet meals. In addition, my income was such that I had a surplus after living expenses. This allowed me to bank most of my salary after I paid the rent on my apartment in Washington. After a few years, I had saved enough money for a down payment on a one-bedroom condominium in Arlington, Virginia.

For the first time in my life, I was now a property owner. This helped my sense of self-esteem and began the long and gradual process of making me feel that America was my home. It's ironic that the seed of that feeling was planted when I was thousands of miles away from mainland US. Maybe that feeling was something like what many US soldiers felt when they fought overseas during World War II: they realized that they were fighting for what they had left behind.

I continued to work for the OIO in Washington, DC, until 1977. During that time, I took numerous trips abroad, including trips to our posts of duty (PODs) in Mexico City, Caracas, Sao Paulo, and Paris. From those PODs, I traveled to other destinations, including Ecuador, Colombia, Guatemala, Panama, Argentina, Spain, and Switzerland. One of my dream trips was to Paris. It was my post of duty for about four and a half months, from early August to mid December 1974. From there I took side trips to Spain, Switzerland, and Italy. I worked out of the US Embassy, visited all the wonderful sites, dined in fine restaurants, and drank great French wines. During the evenings I also studied French at the Alliance Française and picked up enough French to get by.

Another post of duty was Sao Paulo, Brazil. From there, I traveled to Buenos Aires, Argentina, a gorgeous city with broad avenues and wonderful people, although its politics at the time were unsettling, to say the least. It was a time of military control of the government and "*los desaparecidos,*" the disappearances of about 30,000 young men, women, and even children who had defied or were perceived to have defied the government.

General Videla was the head of the military junta in control of the country at the time. He started a campaign called Operation Condor to wipe out left-wing terrorism. But this campaign, which later became known as the "Dirty War," was far worse than the one it was intended to combat. After democracy was restored in 1983, a national commission appointed to investigate the fate of the disappeared uncovered horrific atrocities. Some political dissidents, the commission found, had been heavily drugged and then thrown out of airplanes far out over the Atlantic Ocean, leaving no trace of their passing. Thousands of other civilian dissidents, most unconnected to the left-wing terrorism the military junta was combating, were sent to secret detention centers where they were tortured and murdered. The phrase "*los desaparecidos*" was infamously coined by General Videla, who said in a press conference, "They are neither dead nor alive, they disappeared."

I arrived in Argentina shortly after the junta took power on March 24, 1976. The civilian airport for Buenos Aires was located outside of the city; the one closer to the city was reserved for the military. As we disembarked, we had to walk past soldiers in full uniform spaced fifteen feet apart and holding submachine guns. That was intimidating. We boarded a bus to take us into the city. As we approached the city, I heard a series of shots. I looked out my window and saw a man in a suit running at full speed firing a pistol at someone in front of him. I couldn't see at whom he was firing, but I was glad the bus kept going.

I stayed in Buenos Aires for several days and worked out of the US Embassy. I didn't encounter any problems. In fact, I found the people and my stay very pleasant. But on the last day there, I had a little time left before the embassy car was to take me back to the airport. I decided to walk over to Calle Florida, the famous street with elegant shops and eateries frequented by the rich Argentineans and tourists. It is closed to vehicular traffic and pedestrians enjoy strolling and shopping at leisure. I thought I would stroll around and take some pictures before leaving.

Suddenly, a car drove onto the street and stopped abruptly in the middle, a few feet from me. Two burly men armed with pistols jumped out and walked in my direction. One of them gave me a look that I interpreted as very unfriendly, although he didn't say anything to me. Maybe I was young enough to be seen as a possible dissident, but he must've figured out from my clothing that I was an American. My diplomatic immunity notwithstanding, I thought it prudent to retreat to the Embassy to await my ride. Nothing came of the incident, fortunately, other than my reaffirming the old adage that discretion is the better part of valor.

On another trip, I went to Mexico City and was scheduled to go from there to Guatemala. The embassy staff had reserved a hotel room for me at one of the nicer hotels in Guatemala City, the capitol of Guatemala. The night before I was to leave, the embassy received a flash that the hotel had been bombed, probably by leftist guerrillas. They reserved a room for me at another hotel, but warned me that I should be very careful during this period of political unrest. They told me than an embassy car would pick me up at the airport and take me to the hotel. Any trips thereafter also would be made with an embassy car and driver.

After I landed at the airport in Guatemala City, I walked into the terminal and looked around for the embassy car. I couldn't spot it, and no one seemed to be looking for me. So I took a cab to the hotel, changed my clothes, freshened up, and walked over to the embassy, which was nearby. When I got there, the staff was relieved and upset at the same time. They were relieved that I was OK, but upset that I didn't wait for the embassy car. I didn't think it had been a big deal, but I promised not to take any more unprotected excursions.

The next day, I had to take a trip outside the city to visit a delinquent taxpayer who resided in a smaller town. I was assigned a bulletproof embassy car with a driver and a guard who rode shotgun in the front. It wasn't a shotgun, actually; it looked more like a high-powered rifle, which he kept hidden under the bank seat in front. On the return trip, I asked the driver to stop at a wayside vendor near a small village so I could get a Coke and some snacks. I didn't think the situation was that dangerous and tried to chat briefly in Spanish with the woman vendor. She was polite and sold me the items I requested, but wasn't keen to chat. She and the others with her seemed intimidated by the *gringo* and the two burly men in the large black car.

Since IRS has no jurisdiction outside of the United States, it might seem unusual that we would travel abroad to collect money for the government. While the IRS is very powerful within US borders, it has no authority in foreign countries beyond what is spelled out in its tax treaties with those countries. The treaties, if there are any, require formal and lengthy procedures to be followed in conjunction with the foreign country's tax authorities, and do not permit the type of administrative action authorized within the United States. The IRS rarely used these tax treaty procedures though, except in very large or politically important cases.

Consequently, our authority was very limited. We worked out of US embassies or consulates and contacted the delinquent taxpayers either in person or by phone. We could request payment, but not demand it. Some expatriate taxpayers would be shocked enough by our contact to pay the tax liability voluntarily, although the majority simply declined after the shock of seeing us in a foreign country wore off. We could also gather information if it was a public record, or if it was provided voluntarily.

In one case, I was able to ascertain that a US expatriate living in Mexico had book royalties from the University of Texas Press and was able to collect the money by levying on his US-based royalties. The way it happened is that I telephoned the taxpayer's home in Cuernavaca several times in an effort to speak to him. Each time I called, his wife answered the phone and wouldn't allow me to speak to him. She was protective of him and explained to me that he was a sensitive author who had written a book about native Mexican costumes.

Rather than continue to press the issue, I decided to speak to the wife. She was willing, even eager, to talk about her husband's work.

"You say that your husband is a writer?" I asked.

"Yes, he is."

"You must be very proud of him. What kind of writing does he do?"

"He writes about local Mexican culture and customs. He just published a book on Mexican costumes."

"Really? That's fascinating. Did he publish it in the US, or here in Mexico?"

"In the US, with the University of Texas Press."

"Congratulations again. Please give him my regards."

In the course of the conversation I found out, as I suspected, that the royalties from the book were modest and that she was, in effect, the sole support for the two of them via a trust that had been set up for her by her deceased father.

After the conversation ended, I sent a request to IRS's collection office in Austin, Texas, asking the staff to serve a levy on the University of Texas Press. The levy required that any residual royalties due the author be sent to the IRS. Even though I suspected that the levy proceeds wouldn't pay off the balance of tax due, I hoped that it would embarrass the wife enough to pay her husband's tax bill with money from her dad's trust.

In fact, that's what happened. She called me after the University of Texas Press had informed her of the levy. She said that the IRS levy was deeply embarrassing to her husband and that she would make a special request to her trustee to pay us off. She only asked that we take no further action until she was able to secure the funds.

I didn't have a problem with using this ploy against the nice woman. I saw this as a case of using resourcefulness when I couldn't exercise the power of the government to collect funds that were legally due. And it wasn't as if I were taking money from a destitute taxpayer. Some of the cases I had in Jersey City and other US locations were much closer calls, morally speaking.

At any rate, this job was more interesting than anything I had done before, and the travel was a bonus. I could visit different countries, meet interesting people, and then leave before ennui set in. In addition, I was getting good pay, plus a travel allowance that enabled me to stay at luxury hotels and dine at fine restaurants, all the while banking my salary. What was there not to like? Most young people at the time, I suspect, would've taken this job in a heartbeat.

In retrospect, the travel was more than enjoyably liberating for me; it was almost like a genetic need. I'm not sure there is any such thing, but having been dislodged from my home when I was five, travel felt like a psychic substitute for the home I had lost.

I know that doesn't make sense. How can travel be a substitute for the need to belong? I don't know. Maybe it's something like the concept of going away to find oneself. Maybe it's like a Gypsy/Roma syndrome, if there is any such thing. The Gypsy/Roma are nomads. The majority of their ancestors left India in the eleventh century after the Muslim invasion. Over the next centuries, they dispersed throughout Europe, the

Middle East, North Africa, and the Americas. They've had no land of their own since then and, like the Jews, have been persecuted, enslaved, thrown out, or exterminated by various countries. Like the Jews, the Roma had strong customs and kept to themselves. After the Christian re-conquest of Spain, laws were passed prohibiting Roma dress, language, and customs. They were expelled from Paris in 1539 and had to leave England in 1563 under the threat of death. In the beginning of the fifteenth century, many Roma were forced into slavery by Hungarian and Romanian nobles who needed laborers for their large estates. More recently, the Nazis persecuted them before and during World War II. An estimated 500,000 Roma perished in concentration camps.

So maybe I had some version of the Gypsy/Roma syndrome, although, unlike the Roma, who saw contact with non-Roma as "polluting," I wanted very much to belong and to assimilate into the larger American society.

My efforts to find my identity began to coalesce during this period. Among other things, my social life improved. It wasn't that I had suddenly metamorphosed from a chrysalis to a beautiful butterfly; it was the fact that single women outnumbered the single men in Washington, DC, at that time by a whopping 30 percent. You could hook up with women at night clubs, restaurants, stores, condo buildings, etc. Like men, many of the single women had transferred from out of town and were eager and willing to make friends. The same was true in the various posts of duty I visited. IRS employees were often stationed abroad for months at a time and looked forward to social occasions.

Travel also helped me to get out of my head and broaden my outlook. The good thing about this type of travel was that it was voluntary, not forced as it was in my childhood. The forced expatriation had fractured my sense of self and I felt a need to put the pieces of my psyche back together again.

Another idea I came up with during this period was to revisit the places of my childhood that were etched in my memory. I had some disposable income and I thought such visits would help me to reconnect my past with the present. It was fortuitous that I met Heidi, a beautiful German girl, when I was in the Peace Corps in Ecuador. We dated from time to time and I kept in contact with her over the years after we left Ecuador. Like me, she loved to travel and, from time to time, we would take trips together. On one occasion, we arranged to meet when she was back in Germany. I flew there and she showed me around several places, including Kempten, Allgäu.

It felt strange to be back there after all those years. When Heidi took me to Salzstrasse, a busy commercial street, my thoughts went back to my childhood after the war. I remembered walking on Salzstrasse when I was eight or nine. It was a beautiful summer day. My parents had gone out somewhere and left me alone in the *lager* apartment. Not having supervision, I decided to walk to town by myself to explore.

A German boy, older and bigger than me, recognized me and came up to me as I strolled around. He didn't look too happy. I don't remember why, but he had a distinct dislike of me. Maybe he remembered me from the Halloween fights we Lithuanian boys from the DP camp used to have with the local German boys. It was an annual ritual that started after the war. For some reason, the German boys dressed up as American Indians, replete with feathers and tomahawks. So, naturally, we Lithuanian boys made believe we were cowboys. Besides being opposite of what the German boys were, we liked being cowboys because, as depicted in American movies, the cowboys were "the good guys." We didn't have enough money to buy cowboy clothes, though, so we just made believe we were cowboys.

Dozens of German boys, dressed in full Indian regalia, would gather near the shore of the River Iller and we Lithuanian boys would gather on the other bank and throw rocks at them. I don't know why we threw rocks at them, or why they threw rocks at us. I don't remember who threw the first rocks. It was just a boys' thing to do, I guess. Maybe it was territorial. Maybe it was simple boredom.

At any rate, this big German boy recognized me on Salzstrasse. He took hold of me by the collar and started to lead me away from the busy part of the street. His intentions were not good, I decided. I had to think quickly and assess the situation. Aside from being smaller than he was, I had the additional disadvantage of wearing girls' shoes that were three or four sizes too big. They were the only ones I could find in the apartment after my parents left. On instinct, I turned quickly toward him, punched him rapidly in the stomach, jumped out of the shoes, and ran off as fast as my bare feet could carry me. That spunky move caught him by surprise. In the three or four seconds it took him to recovered his wits, I was gone like the wind, flying back to the DP camp.

As an interesting side note, I learned later that Halloween was not a traditional German celebration before the war. The Germans celebrated *Walpurgisnacht* (night of the witches) and *Martinstag* (St. Martin's Day) around that time of the year, but not Halloween. It became popular after the American occupation, especially among the children. Between the American soldiers and the American movies, Halloween caught on in Germany. It gave the German boys a reason to dress up and have fun, something that was in short supply after the war.

As to why the German boys wanted to dress up as American Indians rather than cowboys, I'm not sure. Maybe they liked the colorful costumes, or maybe the American cowboy movies had a deeper impact on them. After the war, the Germans didn't make too many movies of their own and those American cowboy movies were plentiful and cheap. The Indians were usually the bad guys and, based on the Hollywood ethos, they always lost. Maybe the German youngsters saw the Indians as victims and identified with them subconsciously. Their parents had lost the war to the Allies and the German psyche was fragile at that point. Maybe that's why they identified with the underdogs. Maybe not. It's interesting to speculate, though.

Heidi also took me to the Iller, the main river running through the town. I remembered fishing and swimming there when I was a boy. I remembered a strong rainstorm when the Iller was swollen with rapid, tumbling water. There was some sort of a holiday around that time— maybe it was Oktoberfest—and hundreds of people were gathering in town for the celebration. Many walked across a bridge over the Iller en route to the celebration and, between the pressure of the swollen river, and the weight of the multitude, the bridge collapsed. Many fell into the stream and were killed or injured. That image remained in my mind and I recalled it when Heidi and I looked at the Iller. It was another piece of tile being placed back into the mosaic of my psyche.

***

The travel and the life overseas were enjoyable, but the office situation in Washington, DC, was not. We had hundreds if not thousands of cases of delinquent expatriates and could do little to collect the money due. If it was frustrating to try to collect the money while we were abroad, it was completely ineffectual to try from the office in Washington. All we could do was write letters and make phone calls, most of which were an exercise in futility. It was tedious and boring to do that for eight hours a day in our small and confining office on Fourteenth Street. Most of the revenue officers simply stopped trying and passed the time socializing while they waited for the next assignment abroad. The two first-line managers were complicit in this because, frankly, the goal of collecting the money was largely unobtainable.

Many of the revenue officers had outgoing personalities and enjoyed the social interaction. Greg, for example, could talk for hours on end. He had a good sense of humor, which he blended into the conversations, and was often at the center of social interaction. He rarely did any work, but never had trouble passing the performance reviews; his managers were part of this social circle. Eventually, he was promoted to a management position at another IRS office.

Matt was another likeable employee. He was a good-looking guy in his late twenties or early thirties. He was openly gay, which was uncommon in the late 1970s. Most gays in those days were still afraid to come out of the closet. But Matt had such a likeable personality it was almost impossible to make fun of him, or to make derogatory remarks about his sexual orientation. If someone tried, Matt was no pushover. He knew how to fight back with his lightning-quick wit.

Most of the other revenue officers either were part of this impromptu social circle or knew how to blend in. As usual, I wasn't very good at socializing and sought to stay busy in order to avoid getting involved. I felt somewhat different because of my background and wasn't comfortable with their easy banter and their humorous exchanges based on their middle-class experiences. This tended to isolate me. Maybe they would've accepted me better if I had reached out, but I felt very guarded about my background and was too focused on my career goals. I didn't realize that to advance in a bureaucratic organization, you must also know how to play ball with your fellow workers. I hadn't learned yet to balance the work ethic with the social aspects of the office. In a small environment where the social aspect was magnified, I didn't do very well.

This was a tough environment to work in and I longed to take trips abroad and/or transfer out of IRS's Office of International Operations. My chance came in 1978. I was offered a Grade 12 revenue officer position in Puerto Rico and decided to accept it. I wasn't particularly fond of the idea of moving to Puerto Rico, but at least I was getting out of a very unpleasant situation in Washington, DC. The positive aspect was that the position in Puerto Rico was a promotion with higher pay. The clincher was that the government offered to pick up the tab for transferring my personal belongings, including large-ticket items, such as my car and my furniture.

But my underlying reason for taking the job was deeper. I knew that my options outside of the IRS were not good; they were even worse than inside the IRS. I was thirty-eight—almost thirty-nine—and my prospects in the private world were limited. I could go into private collections, but that didn't appeal to me. So I was stuck with IRS, at least for the foreseeable future. I perceived that my relationship with the IRS defined me as a person. I had tried to define myself after high school, but failed. I tried to define myself again after I ended my Peace Corps assignment, but failed again. Without independent economic resources, a job becomes a big factor in defining who you are. So I had to try to make it inside the IRS. Since the OIO in Washington was a lost cause, I had to go where there was a semblance of opportunity.

In addition, I was getting tired of travel. As much as I had enjoyed it in the past, it was starting to wear thin. The last trip I took at OIO was a marathon. I flew to Mexico City and spent several months there, including side trips to Costa Rica, Panama, and Guatemala. Then I flew to Caracas, Venezuela, where I spent another month, including side trips to Ecuador and Peru. Finally, I flew to Sao Paulo, Brazil, with a side trip to Buenos Aires, Argentina. After the tour was over, I flew back to Mexico City, with a stopover and change of planes in Caracas. The distance between Buenos Aires and Mexico City is about five thousand miles and took about twenty hours, door to door. I left Buenos Aires at three in the afternoon and arrived in Mexico City around noon of the following day, grungy and tired. My efforts to sleep on the planes were only marginally successful.

I checked in at the embassy later that afternoon and heard about a party for the IRS staff that evening. It was being held at the home of the assistant IRS director there. Of course, I couldn't turn down the chance to socialize with the staff. When I got there, I sat down on the couch with Benedictine on the rocks, my favorite drink. I gulped it down and got another one before the first one hit me. I got halfway through it and just conked out on the sofa. About midnight, some of the men at the party hauled me back to my hotel and plopped me on my bed.

The next day I woke up on the floor. It was around noon and I didn't remember how I had gotten there. I stood up to get myself together and almost keeled over. It took a few days to get myself back to a semblance of normality.

So I decided that I'd had enough traveling for a while. I didn't view Puerto Rico as the place where I would settle down, but it was a stepping-stone in that general direction. At least I hoped so.

CHAPTER 20

IRS-PUERTO RICO

I transferred officially to Puerto Rico on January 27, 1978. I wasn't a total stranger there. I had been detailed to Ponce and to the IRS's main office Hato Rey, the business section of San Juan, for month-long stints in 1976 and 1977. It appears that the division chief, who was also in charge of the Puerto Rico office, intended those details to prepare me for possible transfer there in the future. It also gave the employees in Puerto Rico a chance to get acquainted with me—a trial run, of sorts. I passed the test, I guess, because I was awarded the GS-12 revenue officer position in Puerto Rico once the opening came up.

After I got there, I realized that my transfer was controversial with IRS employees in Puerto Rico, especially the managers. They weren't too happy about an "outsider" taking the GS-12 position, which they thought should've gone to one of the locals.

I wasn't thrilled to be there either, but I tried to make the best of it. First and foremost, I looked at it as a great opportunity to play tennis. I had begun to play tennis regularly in Washington, DC, and liked it very much. I was always good athletically, but never developed those skills. Once I started, though, it was like finding a long-lost brother I didn't know I had. I saw my stay in Puerto Rico as a chance to play a lot of tennis and improve my game.

I played mostly at the Carib Inn, a hotel located in the Isla Verde section of San Juan. One reason I liked it there was that I didn't need to organize the matches. I just showed up with my racket. Sooner or later, someone would organize a match with the available players, or look for an extra player because one of the regulars didn't show. In the meantime, I could just sit there and enjoy the sun.

My social life did take a hit, though. Dating was not as free there as it was in Washington. This was surprising, especially since there seemed to be a dichotomy between the openly feminine way many of the young women dressed and the conservative way they behaved with men. It reminded me of the 1950s culture back in the states. When I was growing up, in my neighborhood, at least, if we saw a girl all dolled up, we figured she was looking for action; the "good girls" didn't dress that way. They ignored us if we weren't polite to them.

So when I tried to strike up conversations with pretty young women in Puerto Rico, I was often surprised by how they reacted. This seemed to be especially true with the single young women from the more educated middle- and/or higher-class social groups. They were family oriented and didn't date just anyone they ran into at a nightclub; they had to be introduced properly to a suitor, who also would be closely scrutinized by her family. Since I wasn't rich or socially connected, I didn't date many local young women.

Ironically, Puerto Rico is where I met my future wife. I guess there's something to be said for such a dating culture. Our meeting was accidental—literally. It was entirely my fault. I made a badly timed and careless U-turn on Roosevelt Road in the Hato Rey section of greater San Juan and another car hit me. The citation from the police officer required me to appear in court. I sought an attorney to represent me and contacted one that I knew at the offices where I worked. She said she couldn't represent me because she worked for the federal government, but gave me the name and phone number of Margarita Marchan Cuevas, a friend of hers and a local attorney in private practice. I called Margarita and made an appointment to see her at her office.

Margarita was attractive and seemed friendly beyond the professional attorney/client relationship. I made a note to ask her out after the legal proceedings were concluded. She agreed to represent me and appeared with me in court. The judge let me off with a relatively modest fine, which was reasonable under the circumstances. I guess Margarita did a good job.

This added gratitude to her attractiveness and I invited her for dinner to celebrate the successful outcome. We dated on and off thereafter. She was thirty-three, six years younger than I was. Both of her parents were deceased and her one sister, who was married to an American, had moved to California. So maybe her scrutiny of me as a potential suitor was less intense than that of other local women would have been. However, I was single, never married, Roman Catholic, and spoke Spanish. That was enough to open the door and overcome the social and cultural differences between us.

I enjoyed our dates, but in all honesty, I didn't see her as a future wife at the time. My top choices were still a Lithuanian girl first, and an American second; Lithuanian-American would've been perfect. Puerto Rican women were never serious contenders for my wonderful and exclusive affection (yeah, right!), although Margarita was start-ing to make me waver. Maybe her friendliness, my age, and the won-derfully sensual tropical climate of Puerto Rico had something to do with it.

Apart from Margarita, my social life was still fairly limited—part-ly because I didn't have the rich, white, American "gringo" stereotype image going for me the way I did in Ecuador and other parts of Latin America. Puerto Rico had a long history with America already and I wasn't perceived as some exotic transplant from the land of plenty. While it's true that the Puerto Rican culture and language were, and still are, predominantly Hispanic, American influence on the island had grown over the years. By the time I arrived there, the overwhelming majority of Puerto Ricans wanted a political affiliation with the United States, either in some version of its status as a commonwealth, or as the fifty-first state of the union.

During my stay in Puerto Rico, however, I didn't forget my long-term goal of visiting the places of my childhood in order to reconnect to my past. I reestablished ties with Maryte Tendžegolskiené, nee Gružauskaité, a cousin on my mother's side, who lived in Lithuania. Unlike us, her family decided to remain in Lithuania after the second Soviet occupa-tion in 1944. I guess they managed to survive without being killed or sent to the Russian Gulag in Siberia. She invited me to visit her and, to my surprise, I learned that I could—even though Lithuania was still under Soviet Communist rule. The Russian government must've made an economic decision to open the country to tourism in order to bring in US dollars despite its paranoia toward Western democracy. On May 8, 1978, I flew to Moscow and from there to Vilnius, Lithuania. This was my first time back in Lithuania since we left in October 1944.

When we landed at the airport in Vilnius, Maryte, her husband, and their two daughters, Valyté and Nyjolé, stood silently on the tarmac with other locals, waiting to greet the arrivals. They all held tulips, which, I gathered, was the traditional form of greeting. The thing that struck me most about the scene was the complete and polite stillness of the people. Having traveled considerably over the last several years, I had become conditioned to the bustle and animation of people in airports all over the world. I was surprised by how somber the people were at the airport in Vilnius. All I could think of was that thirty-four years of Communist rule must've instilled a sad obedience in them, or possibly a fear of being demonstrative. Demonstrative people tend to be conspicuous, which is dangerous in a dictatorship. It made me think about how grateful I was that Dad had made the courageous decision to leave Lithuania, notwithstanding the dislocation and hardship we endured thereafter.

I made an effort to be cheerful, speaking the best Lithuanian I could muster. It took some effort. Even though Lithuanian was my native tongue, there had been long stretches in the previous ten years when I barely spoke it at all. People in some of the places I'd lived or visited had never heard of Lithuania. But Maryté and her family were happy to see me and were forgiving of my lack of fluency. Family connections are stronger than words and we had no problem understanding each other almost immediately. They were especially grateful for the gifts I brought them, including blue jeans for the daughters (a prized item at the time) and some hard American dollars for Maryté.

After checking into the Intourist Hotel, I was able to rent a car to drive to the city of Kaunas where Maryté and her family lived. There were several conditions attached: first, I couldn't drive the car myself; it had to be driven by an authorized chauffeur. Second, I couldn't spend the night in Kaunas; I had to come back to my hotel in Vilnius the same day.

The "chauffeur" was a government employee who kept an eye on me to make sure that I didn't do anything subversive, like be nice to my relatives. As the chauffeur drove to Kaunas on the expressway, he pointed to other cars heading in the same direction and told Maryté and me that those motorists lacked official permission. It wasn't clear to me how he knew that—if he did—but he made it a point to inform us that he was memorizing the makes of the cars and their license plate numbers.

This was disconcerting and unpleasant. I decided that he wasn't going to intimidate me. I was a US citizen, I told myself, protected by the US Embassy. After we arrived in Kaunas, I told the driver to get lost and pick me up about 6 p.m. for the trip back to Vilnius. He didn't like my insurrectionist tone of voice, but left us alone when I went into Maryté's home. He waited for me at the downtown plaza, but gave Maryté and me the evil eye when we walked by during a sightseeing tour of the town.

Maryté's mother, the wife of my mom's brother, Juazas, cooked a wonderful dinner in my honor with all the traditional Lithuanian dishes, including *kotlietai, cepelinai, kugelis,* and *bulviniai blynai.* I ate to my heart's content. I ate until I thought I would burst. It reminded me of the feast we had for Henry's christening in 1944. The thing I remember most about this feast was that the dishes tasted precisely the way Mom used to make them. Over the years, I had eaten some of those dishes in various places and on various occasions, such Lithuanian picnics, but they never tasted exactly the same as Mom's. Here, I had traveled more than five thousand miles and made a visceral connection to the essence of my childhood. That's probably as close as I ever got to reconnecting with that distant, but unforgettable past.

I inquired about traveling to Plungé, the town where I was born, but was told in no uncertain terms that it would not be possible. I was disappointed but not surprised. Apparently, it was off limits. They didn't want tourists nosing around small towns where Soviet officials had less control, apparently, and where the poverty and oppression were more evident.

I left Lithuania somewhat disappointed. While I had made a momentary connection to my roots via the feast they prepared for me, I didn't have the "aha" moment I had hoped for. It was probably naïve of me to think that I would. First, I wasn't able to go to Plungé, the mecca of my roots. Second, Lithuania was still under Soviet Communist rule. I couldn't feel unshackled from my past, I thought, until Lithuania was free again. That was the reason we'd left thirty-four years earlier. Finally, I still had my struggles in America, the land to which I wanted to belong. My life in America had very little to do with Lithuania, but I was hoping to somehow make the emotional connection between them.

So I went back to the tropical island of Puerto Rico and remained there until October 1980. My chance to return to the US mainland came when a friend from the OIO office came on an official visit from Washington, DC. She had been a revenue officer when I was there, although by that time she had been promoted to staff assistant for the collection division chief who had jurisdiction over the IRS office in Puerto Rico. I was happy to see her and told her that things were not working out for me in Puerto Rico. I asked her to see if I could be transferred back to the United States. She conveyed this message to her boss, who was able to get me a lateral transfer to Chicago. He even managed to get the Chicago office to pick up the cost of moving my personal belongings. I sold my beautiful condo on the twenty-second floor of a highrise in the Miramar section of San Juan and left for Chicago on October 17, 1980. I didn't realize at the time that my connection to Puerto Rico wouldn't be broken as easily as that.

CHAPTER 21
IRS–CHICAGO

I was over forty years old and tired of bouncing around the world. I decided to make my final stand in Chicago. It was as good a place as any; maybe better. I thought I might reconnect with the Lithuanian community in Chicago, the largest in the United States, although that was more of a social goal rather than a priority. My priority was still my career and I thought I would try one more time to make it within the IRS. The manager of the group to which I was assigned saw some potential in me and helped to guide me onto a managerial track.

I also decided to take another stab at defining myself. For the past ten years or so, I had thought of attending law school. I knew that law school would broaden my career options, but I wasn't sure I could get in. My college grades weren't that great, and doing well on the LSAT was another challenge. I had made a half-hearted effort once before and got a mediocre score. It was probably not high enough to get me into law school, so I didn't even try. This time, I boned up on the sample questions for the LSAT test in earnest and did better. I applied to the

John Marshall Law School and was accepted. I was thrilled. Regardless of whether things worked out at the IRS, a law degree would add another dimension to my resume. The challenge, though, would be to graduate and pass the bar exam. I wasn't sure I could do it.

I started law school in September 1981. I had to do it in the evenings, of course; I didn't have the economic resources to go to school full time. If I took some summer courses, I'd be able to finish in four years.

Monday through Thursday evenings at 5:00 p.m., I would leave the IRS's office in downtown Chicago and go across the street to the John Marshall building on Plymouth Court. There, I'd study until classes started at 6:00 p.m. or take a power nap if I was tired. The classes were from 6:00 to 9:00 p.m., including the summer months. I spent ten or twelve hours a day in the library on Saturdays and Sundays, mostly reading case law. That was the way law was taught in those days—and probably is today. You started with actual case law and learned to extrapolate theory from that, not the other way around.

The schedule was brutal, but I was motivated. A lifetime of failures, false starts, and disappointments had instilled a bedrock of determination in me that wouldn't quit. This was my last chance. Thank God for my good health; I couldn't have survived without it.

I did OK in law school—not spectacularly, but well enough to pass the courses. I actually enjoyed some courses and got good grades in them. After two years, I realized I could make it.

My career at the IRS was also starting to take off. Better late than never, I thought. Thanks to the efforts of my manager, I was selected for the IRS's management cadre, although that wasn't a totally smooth process. Here's the story.

Before I became a manager, I conducted a seizure on a garage business that was delinquent in its payroll taxes. It was a routine seizure and one of many I'd conducted throughout my career with the IRS. Per regulations, I submitted the required documents and reports of the seizure to a reviewer, whose job was to make sure that I'd followed proper procedures. The reviewer sent back a request for additional documents and/or information. Parts of his request were nonsensical, I thought, and seemed to indicate that he didn't have a good understanding of how seizures were conducted. My perception was that I was following the IRS policy of aggressive enforcement and doing the nitty-gritty work in the field, while he was just a bureaucratic pencil-pusher insisting that I dot the "i"s and cross the "t"s. I sent some of the additional documentation he had requested, but added a few snippety comments about the parts of his request that appeared unnecessary and logically self-evident.

Well, this reviewer didn't take kindly to my tone of voice. He decided to teach me a lesson. He referred me to Internal Audit, alleging that the execution of the seizure was improper. Internal Audit investigates dishonesty, fraud, bribes, and other improprieties by IRS employees. The employees feared it greatly because it investigated even the most inane complaints, something left over from the 1950s when this department was formed to combat corruption. What employee doesn't make mistakes from time to time, or take technical shortcuts due to a heavy workload—especially if he is pressured by his manager to move cases promptly?

So Internal Audit opened an official investigation of my seizure and required me to file additional reports and explanations. They interviewed the seized taxpayer, the reviewer, my manager, and me. Everything was documented for the official record. This unpleasant drama went on for months. The upshot: a written reprimand that would be included in my personnel file.

The chief of the Collection Division called me into his office and asked me to sign the written reprimand. My options were to sign it or file a grievance through the union, seeking to overturn the reprimand. I hesitated, but agreed to sign it. It was the mildest form of punishment possible and I thought it best to accept it, under the circumstances. The reprimand was for technical omissions rather than any form of intentional misconduct, and I wanted to put an end to this distraction. I wanted to go on with my life—including focusing on law school. Law school was very demanding of my time and energy and would be my ticket out of the IRS bureaucracy, if push came to shove.

Here's the ironic part: at the end of the meeting, the Collection Division chief offered his hand and informed me that I had been selected for the Management Cadre. I didn't know whether to laugh or cry. This was bureaucratic office politics at its best.

At any rate, I was starting to feel pretty good about myself, and about the direction my life was taking. But one large gap remained: I still needed to put my personal life in order. My goal was to hook up with a nice, Lithuanian girl who had been born and raised in the United States. I thought that would tie my past neatly to the present. But the prospects weren't promising. There was one woman whom I really liked, but she didn't like me. Another one, from my generation and my type of background, was very interested in me, but I didn't like her. She was too "old school," I felt. I wanted someone who had Lithuanian roots, but was firmly planted in the American culture.

My second plan for matrimony, to find an American woman, wasn't looking good either. The ones I knew and dated had personal issues that kept them from making a commitment—somewhat like I did, I guess. My chances had been better in Washington, DC, where the odds and the dating culture were much better.

I began to re-examine my social goals. Perhaps they were unrealistic, I thought; maybe they were never meant to be. Perhaps, like Miguel Cervantes's Don Quixote, I was chasing windmills. I started to use my brain instead of the nostalgia that was deeply ingrained in me from childhood. Maybe I wanted a Lithuanian girl in order to recapture the culture and the identity I had lost when we were forced to abandon Lithuania. That was certainly understandable, maybe even laudable, but was it realistic any longer? My life had taken many turns since we left Lithuania. I had moved on. Was it possible to turn the clock back to a warm and idealistic world that no longer seemed to exist for me? My time for recapturing that part of my life seemed to have passed. Maybe it was never meant to be. Life goes on, some say, and you can never go back.

So I decided to hook up with Margarita again. I was definitely attracted to her and we seem to have a lot in common. We were close in age. Like me, she had never been married. Like me, she was Catholic and had good moral values. What's wrong with thinking outside the emotional box, I asked myself.

We had dated on and off after I left Puerto Rico. Either I would fly there, or she would visit Chicago. In December 1982, when I had some time off from law school for the Christmas holidays, I asked her to come to Chicago.

The weather couldn't have been more cooperative. It was a fluke warm spell with temperatures in the sixties. People were jogging in shorts along the lakefront in Evanston, where I had purchased a small condo. For someone who had been born and raised in a tropical climate,

I guess Margarita decided that Chicago weather wasn't as bad as it was made out to be. When I got down on my knees and proposed to her, she said yes.

After we married, that fateful Christmas holiday was a source of great humor to us and to our friends. Everyone thought I had lured her out of the tropics and fooled her into thinking that Chicago had mild weather. It was made more ironic by the fact that after we married and she moved to Chicago, we had a series of record low temperatures. One night it bottomed out at twenty-eight degrees below zero Fahrenheit, with the wind chill factor pushing the apparent temperature down to minus eighty-one degrees. I think it's still a record.

The condo building we lived in wasn't of the highest construction quality and thick ice formed inside the sills of the north-facing windows. The head of our bed rested against an outside wall and we could actually feel the wind gusts, sending waves of cold through our blanketed and shivering bodies. Margarita slept with a hooded gym parka over her nightclothes. It finally occurred to us to put the head of the bed against an inside wall. That helped somewhat, although it took Margarita many years to acclimate herself to Chicago winters. She still tells me on some winter nights that she should've insisted on a prenuptial agreement with a weather clause.

Our daughters were born one after another, four of them in a period of six years. Maybe those cold winter nights made us snuggle a little closer. Either that or we were making up for lost time. I was forty-four when we married; she was thirty-eight. Everyone in my family was sure that I was a confirmed bachelor; she was an old maid, known affectionately in Spanish as a *jamona*. She was thirty-nine when Clarissa, our oldest, was born. When the labor pains started, I drove her from Evanston to the Prentiss Women's Hospital in downtown Chicago, where Dr. Asher, her OB/GYN doctor, awaited us. It was May 30, 1984, a beautiful spring morning. We were driving south on Lake Shore Drive as the sun crept slowly behind the moon in a full solar eclipse. That seemed like a wonderful omen—and a source of much ribbing of Clarissa as she got older. We told her she had to live up to very high expectations because of the full solar eclipse.

Camille was born fourteen months later, on August 5, 1985. Her birth wasn't as smooth as Clarissa's. Camille was a big baby, almost ten pounds, and getting her through the birth canal wasn't easy. Mom's water broke about 4:30 p.m. and she started to dilate rapidly. We didn't have time to take her to Prentiss. She was fully dilated within an hour and lay in a semi trance on the bed in our condo in Evanston. The paramedics arrived promptly after we dialed 911. We also called Dr. Asher and told her what was going on. She realized that there was no way we could get Margarita to Prentiss Hospital in time and suggested that the paramedics deliver the baby in the apartment. But the paramedics seemed very unsure of themselves and we all stood around like pall bearers, not really knowing what to do. Finally, Margarita roused herself from the trance and shouted in a loud and unmistakable voice, "Get me to the hospital *now!*"

That was the trigger. The paramedics lifted Margarita on to a gurney, shoved her into the ambulance, and rushed her to nearby Evanston Hospital with the sirens wailing. I jumped in my car and followed as fast as I could. They got her to the emergency room where the resident doctor on duty proceeded to take charge of the delivery. There was no time to dress her in a hospital gown or even to transfer her to the operating table. I put on a gown and hospital slippers over my shoes and hurried into the operating room. I held Margarita's hand as Jay Levin, the resident doctor, performed an episiotomy on her—without the local anesthesia. There was no time for it.

Margarita had a delayed reaction to the episiotomy. She was overwhelmed with a maelstrom of feelings and physical pain and didn't sense this very painful cut until several seconds later. Then she let out a yelp and squeezed my hand so hard I cringed. When Camille's head came out, it was purple and bruised, but Margarita couldn't push her out. Camille's shoulders were too big. There was a chance that the doctor would have to break her collarbones. The doctor grabbed hold of Camille's head and twisted it ninety degrees. Slowly, Camille's body followed the direction of the twist until her shoulders were vertically aligned with Mom's enlarged opening. With another abdominal push from Mom, Camille emerged. She was screaming bloody murder, but her shoulders were intact.

The doctor then put his arm inside Margarita, up to his elbow, and pulled out the afterbirth. Margarita let out another painful shout and squeezed my hand mightily. At this point, I started to get woozy. The doctor took notice of my wobbly posture and ordered the nurse to bring me a stool. Margarita had the strength to stay conscious throughout the process, without sedation and without an epidural. She said she took courage from the fact that Dr. Asher knew Jay Levin, the resident doctor at Evanston Hospital, and spoke highly of him.

In spite of the difficulty of the delivery, the one good thing about it was that Camille was born exactly on her due date. If she'd been born even a week earlier, it would've been a lot more complicated. I had graduated from law school that June, completed the two-month bar preparation course, and taken the two-day bar exam only several days before. It had been a very intense several months. Camille's birth in the middle of it would've thrown a wrench into our tight schedule—and probably into my sanity. Either we were lucky or someone up there was keeping an eye on us.

I continued to work for IRS, hoping to get into IRS's legal department, or be offered some other promotion. It didn't happen. The new division chief seemed to have a low opinion of me. He nixed any efforts I made to advance within the IRS. Even though some other managers liked me, apparently the Collection division chief had the final say. He made it clear that he wanted me out.

After a while, I decided to leave the IRS. My last day was August 28, 1986. It was one of the toughest financial decisions I ever made. I had been poor as a child, so I knew I could survive; but it wasn't just me anymore. I now had a wife and two children who depended on me. I was forty-seven years old, not quite the up-and-coming young attorney whom law firms were seeking—if they were hiring at all. The only job offer I got was with a small law firm in Chicago at a rate of pay lower than I had been making at the IRS. In addition, we had purchased a new home in Lisle, Illinois, and the mortgage payments were higher than the ones for the small condominium in Evanston.

It wasn't long before my worst fears of financial insecurity were realized. In March 1987, about six months after I began working for the law firm, it let me go. I was on my own with no job prospects. Our meager safety net was the remains of the $20,000 I had taken out of my IRS retirement fund. After fifteen years at IRS, I took out everything I had put into it. Since I drew it out before I was eligible to retire, I received no more than what I had put in—not even one penny of interest.

Having no other options, I decided to go out on my own. I subleased a small space in the office of another attorney. It was really just an empty storage space the size of a closet and I had to walk through the attorney's office to get to it. It did have a desk and a chair, though, so I was off and running.

I mobilized what brain cells I had left into a game plan. I had IRS experience and I knew there were thousands of delinquent taxpayers in the Chicago area who needed help in dealing with the IRS. All I had to do was let them know that I was qualified and available to help.

To get myself known, I joined several bar associations in the area and offered to write article on tax issues. They were accepted and published in various bar journals. I also joined some committees and spoke on tax issues at seminars. I placed ads in local phone books and mailed brochures to taxpayers in the surrounding counties against whom the IRS had filed liens.

All of those steps helped to get the word out about me and to attract some clients. I also expanded into bankruptcy law. I was well versed in bankruptcy since I had managed the IRS's insolvency units at the Chicago office for several years. Also, bankruptcy was a good option for a number of my tax clients who were struggling financially. Some IRS income tax obligations can be discharged in bankruptcy.

Things were tough at first. The income I earned from the practice was barely enough to pay the office expenses. I didn't draw any wages for the first six months. I paid the mortgage and covered food and other personal expenses from the dwindling IRS retirement fund. In September of that year, we found out that Margarita was pregnant again. The baby was due the next April.

CHAPTER 22
HOME SWEET HOME

The third child, little Margarita, was born on April 29, 1988. Shortly after delivery, the nurse cleaned her, bundled her up, and handed her to me. She stopped crying as I held her, and seemed to be resting after coming into this strange new environment.

"Hi, little Margarita," I said gently. "Happy birthday."

She stirred in response to my voice and turned her head slowly, laboriously, to look at the source of the sound.

"We're happy to see you," I said, trying out my biggest smile.

When her head was facing mine, she opened her eyes and gave me a brief but unmistakable smile.

I melted. From what I knew, babies weren't supposed to smile for several months.

I can't say that we had planned this pregnancy, or that we were logical about these family issues, but there was no way we were *not* going to have the baby. Financial difficulties notwithstanding, every child was a blessing at our ages. Ariana, our fourth and final baby, was born on

September 7, 1990, when Mom was forty-five. She liked to joke thereafter that Ariana was her "last egg." Thank God they were all healthy.

Mom Margarita's ideal was to stay at home and raise the children with close parental supervision, but financial reality put pressure on this ideal. It also dawned on her after several years that raising small children without help is a daunting task. She considered working part time to earn at least enough money to pay for a live-in housekeeper who would clean, cook, and help with the children. But she didn't want to work unless it was at the professional level to which she was accustomed. She was already licensed in Puerto Rico and would only need to pass the Illinois bar exam in order to become licensed to practice law in Illinois.

To prepare for it, she got some bar preparation books and began to study on her own. It was early November 1989. After I came home from work in the evenings, she'd pick up the books and go to one of several libraries in the western suburbs. To break up the monotony of studying, she alternated between them: Lisle Library, Naperville Library, Benedictine University, Northern Illinois, etc. She wouldn't come home until late at night. She even spent some weekends studying.

In the meantime, Margarita had asked Shirley, a retired grandmother who lived across the street, to help with the kids for a few hours a day until I came home from the office. Clarissa and Camille were in kindergarten and preschool and didn't come home until the afternoon, so the one needing the most attention was little Margarita. After I came home, I took over from Shirley. I would warm up Chef Boyardee Tic Tac Toes for them. They seem to like them, and it was easier than trying to cook.

Clarissa and Camille seemed to take Mom's absence in stride; little Margarita, who was only two and a half, had a harder time of it. She had been a model child up until then: even-tempered and low-maintenance.

With Mom's absence, she seemed to lose her sense of self; she started acting up and became more demanding of attention. I didn't know how to handle that.

On January 2, 1990, Mom Margarita started the formal bar-preparation course at the Kent College of Law in downtown Chicago. It lasted almost two months. She took the train there every day. Halfway through the course, she found out she was pregnant with Ariana, our fourth child. During the two-day bar exam, she munched on crackers to keep the nausea down.

She had to wait several months to find out if she passed it, so she went back to focusing on the children in the meantime. It didn't take much detective work to realize that the children needed some motherly attention. They were starting to outgrow their clothes; the sneakers I had been putting on little Margarita every day for the past several months were a full size too small. At least part of her crankiness must've been due to the undersized shoes.

In 1993, when little Ariana was two, Margarita hired a full-time housekeeper. Maria was about sixty at the time and had raised ten children of her own in Mexico. She cleaned the house, cooked, and took care of the children. She had a no-nonsense manner with the girls. They obeyed her, of course, but when they grew up, they told us that they'd held mock trials in the basement of the house and convicted Maria *in absentia* of child abuse and other horrendous crimes. Clarissa, the instigator of these "trials," made sure that the judge showed no mercy, especially in sentencing.

Mom Margarita then opened a law office in Aurora where she helped mostly Hispanic clients who came to see her with miscellaneous legal problems involving traffic violations, family issues, real estate transactions, etc. She didn't earn a lot to begin with, but what she made helped with the household expenses, especially with children's clothing and their other needs. The income from my practice had improved by then and we started to establish ourselves financially.

We flew to New Jersey to visit my parents several times. They were both retired and living on the South Jersey shore. They liked my wife from the first time they met her and loved to dote on their grandchildren. But we could not make these trips very often. Also they were getting on in years already and their health started to deteriorated. The last time we visited, Mom was in a nursing home. I found her sitting alone at a round table in the back of a crowded "social room." When I sat down beside her, she didn't recognize me. She seemed to be in a world of her own. I held her hand and cried. She seemed to respond momentarily. I don't know if she had a glimmer of recognition or simply was responding, as any mother would, to this universal show of human emotion. She died October 10, 1988. She was eighty-two. She'd had a hard life.

Dad died six years later, on September 6, 1994. Several days before, we got a call from my brother Ray who said Dad was in bad shape and probably wouldn't survive. I flew to New Jersey with the entire family to see him. My brother John, and sister Maria flew in from California with some of their families. We went to see him at the hospital. He was suffering from stomach cancer that had metastasized into some of his other vital organs. Tubes were sticking out of his mouth and nose. He couldn't speak, but, unlike Mom, his eyes were ablaze with alertness and recognition of our presence.

He had lost a lot of weight, although his face was bloated from various medications. It was hard to recognize him at first, but there was no mistaking his strong arms. They were still as large and strong as I remembered them. I called them "tree trunks."

We all stood around his bed, not knowing what to do or say. Being the stupid one, I coaxed my older brothers into singing a song that was popular in the DP camp in Kempten. It was a German drinking song called *Trink'n Wir Noch 'n Tröpfchen*, which translates to "Let's Have Another Little Drop." We DPs in Germany added Lithuanian lyrics to the music to poke fun of each other. As I remembered it, it went something like this: "All the dogs are barking, all the dogs are barking, except (insert name) is barking *not*."

So when we started to sing it to Dad that day and got to the part where the name was inserted, I pointed gleefully to John at first and we sang it with John's name. John was the oldest, the favorite of our parents, and it was only fitting that we would make fun of him first. We then repeated the verses with Ray and me taking our turns being joshed.

It was a dumb song and a dumb time to sing it, but Dad's eyes twinkled in recognition. When the song stopped and we lost our mustered enthusiasm to sing any more, I looked at Dad and said, "You can let go now, Dad. We love you."

My voice broke and I choked up as I said it. In retrospect, maybe it was stupid thing to say, but it was instinctive. I didn't remember ever standing in front of a dying man before, much less my father, and hadn't thought of what to say.

We left that evening to go back to our homes in California and Chicago, but I knew we would be back in a day or two to bury him. On the flight home, I thought about one of the few times Dad and I had had a nonconfrontational conversation. It was a Saturday morning in Elizabeth. I had just finished breakfast at the Formica kitchen table that had been in our family for more than twenty years and was enjoying a cup of coffee. He sat down across from me and somehow the conversation got around to smoking. I had already quit, but he was still smoking a pack or two a day.

"How long has it been since you quit smoking?" he asked.

"Three or four years, maybe," I answered.

"Was it hard to quit?"

"It wasn't bad. I'd quit a few times before, so I knew what to expect."

"Are you sure you won't take it up again?"

"Yeah, I'm pretty sure. The last few times I just wanted to see if I could do it."

"Well, I have to give you credit for being able to do it. It takes a lot of will power."

It was one of the few times I can remember that Dad gave me a compliment. That softened me up a little and we continued to chat.

"I still get the urge once in a while," I said, "like when I go drinking, or when I'm having my morning coffee like this."

"I can quit, too, you know," Dad said, out of the blue.

I smiled at him and expressed my doubt. "Dad, you've been smoking for thirty or forty years. How many packs a day do you smoke?"

"At least one, sometimes two or three."

"That's what I mean. I can't believe you could quit now."

"I'll bet you I can."

"I don't think you're serious."

"How much do you want to bet?"

I thought I would humor him and offered to bet him five dollars.

"Come on," he said. "Make it worth my while." He was still smiling.

"OK," I said. "Let's make it twenty. But I'm not sure how I'll be able to monitor you. I can't watch you twenty-four hours a day."

"I give you my word," he said. "I will not cheat."

And he didn't. To my knowledge, he never smoked again until the day he died. I never paid him the twenty dollars he earned. He never asked for it.

The Requiem Mass for him was held at Saints Peter and Paul's Church in Elizabeth, New Jersey, and presided over by Father Alfred Zemeikis. As the Mass droned on, we, his children, sat huddled in a small group, and I began to cry. The crying turned into sobbing. I was embarrassed that I couldn't control myself. It lasted about ten or fifteen minutes. No one looked at me the entire time; I felt grateful for that.

My father had been a hard man; I had loved and hated him at the same time. When I stopped sobbing, I felt better. Those were tears of release and, in his death, I was reconciled with my father.

***

On March 11, 1990, the Lithuanian government issued a proclamation declaring its independence from the Soviet Union. The seeds of this independence proclamation were sown with the reforms started by Mikhail Gorbachev, who assumed the office of the General Secretary of the Communist Party of the Soviet Union in March 1985. Shortly thereafter, he started the political and economic reforms known as "perestroika" and "glasnost" in an effort to modernize this vast and cumbersome Russian empire. Lithuanians enthusiastically jumped on these reform efforts and organized the Lithuanian Reconstruction Movement in 1988. This organization subsequently became known in Lithuania as Sajudis. It was led by Vytautas Landsbergis, a professor of musicology, who was not a member of the Communist party. Sajudis gained political power by electing representatives to the newly authorized Congress of People's Deputies and helped to elect Algirdas Brazauskas as its first secretary of the Communist Party in Lithuania. Brazauskas cooperated with Landsbergis and Sajudis, resulting in the declaration of independence from the Soviet Union on March 11, 1990.

At first, Gorbachev didn't accept the legality of this declaration and imposed an economic blockade that lasted three months. Moscow also obstructed Lithuanian efforts to gain Western recognition and, on January 3, 1991, attempted to reestablish Soviet rule by use of military force. Soviet troops forcibly took over the TV Tower in Vilnius killing, in the process, at least thirteen unarmed civilians and injuring about 700 who attempted to resist. Other civilians erected barricades around Seimas, the Lithuanian parliament, in an effort to prevent the Soviet troops from taking control of it. The worldwide media coverage of the events seemed to help. Moscow backed off from any further acts to crush the independence movement and the troops returned to their barracks.

Subsequent political events within the Soviet Union itself, including the failed coup against the Gorbachev government on August 19, 1991, resulted in the demise of the Soviet Union and, by the fall of 1991, Lithuania's government gained recognition from other countries and the United Nations.

Lithuania reorganized itself politically into a European-style parliamentary democracy and transitioned from a centrally planned economy to a free market economy. The withdrawal of the last Russian troops was completed by August 31, 1993. In 2004, Lithuania joined the European Union and the North Atlantic Treaty Organization. After six decades of Communist domination, Lithuania was free again.

In June 2003, I decided to visit Lithuania once again. Unlike my first visit in 1978, it was now independent of the brutal shackles imposed by the Soviet Union and I was anxious to see what changes had taken place. I thought of the visit as a closing of the circle of my peripatetic life. Perhaps it would help to merge the pieces of my fragmented psyche.

I was a member of an association of US attorneys of Lithuanian descent, known as the Lithuanian American Bar Association. Its leaders organized a joint conference with attorneys in Lithuania and I was scheduled to speak there on US bankruptcy laws. I coordinated my presentation with Jurgita Spaiciene, a Lithuanian law student at Kaunas University, who was to speak on bankruptcy laws in Lithuania.

At the urging of my wife, I decided to bring my entire family. She wanted our four daughters, who were teenagers or about to be, to get a feel for Dad's roots.

It was a wonderful reunion with the land of my birth. We_visited Seimas and met the chairman in his office. We also ran into Mr. Landsbergis, the leader and spiritual head of Sajudis. We walked around old town Vilnius, one of the largest surviving medieval old towns in Northern Europe, with its winding cobblestone streets and buildings of Gothic, Renaissance, Baroque, and neoclassical styles of architecture. The government had begun major restorations and it was becoming a significant tourist attraction. My wife Margarita loved it. It reminded her of Old San Juan in her native land of Puerto Rico. She especially loved the beautiful, traditional jewelry that has been made for many centuries from amber that washes up on the shores of the Baltic Sea.

After the conference was over, we rented a large French car, something between a station wagon and an SUV, and drove to Plungé, the town where I was born. The first sight we saw as we approached the town was the railroad station from which our family had left in haste, fear, and uncertainty almost sixty years before. It was surreal, like an out-of-body experience. I didn't know what I felt, or what I was supposed to feel. My vague plan was to see, if possible, the house where we used to live, one of the few things I could still vaguely remember about Plungé. My cousin Maryté took us to a street in town where she thought our house used to stand, although she wasn't sure. The house was no longer there. I learned that many of those old-style homes had been demolished after the Russians occupied Lithuania. So Clarissa picked up a pebble from the spot where we thought the house had been and brought it back to America. I guess it was as good a memento as any considering what little we had to go by.

I came back to Plungé again three years later with my wife, my oldest brother John, and his wife, Marion. John was twelve when we left in 1944 and I thought he might remember the location of our house better than Maryté did. We came pretty close, I think. John remembered walking Mom's beloved cow to the pasture in Oginskis Park every morning. The park and the gate were still there and we were able to retrace his steps to where he thought the house had stood. We narrowed the location down to a small, triangular park, which is there now. We took a few pictures of it with me pointing to the sign identifying the park.

That's about as close as I got to reconnecting to that distant, almost mythical past of my childhood. Did I reconnect the pieces of my fragmented psyche? Maybe not the way I had imagined, or hoped I would, but it helped.

The psyche is more complex than just one's roots. I began to accept the fact that my world had moved on in new and unexpected directions and that one can never go back and recapture completely what has been lost. I now had a new life, a new family, a new occupation. I also had learned to accept myself, warts and all, and to love who I was. I had made it as an immigrant in the nation of immigrants and I was now an American. The process wasn't smooth—not like it's made out to be in books and movies. It was more like making sausages: the process isn't pretty, but the final product tastes good.

The land and culture of my birth will be with me until I die, but now I have a new land and a new culture that I love. More importantly, I have found myself and that has made me realize that my heart is big enough for both. Lithuania belongs to the people who live there and to those who survived the hardships of the past sixty years. I survived the hardships of the diaspora and the acculturation to the new land where I now belong.

God Bless Lithuania. God Bless America.

Left to right: brother Ray, author, brother John; circa 2009.

APPENDIX

THE MARIACHI MASS IN THE CATHEDRAL OF CUERNAVACA

By Tony Mankus

August 11, 1967

At ten o'clock, an hour before the Mass is scheduled to begin, several people are already inside the cathedral. Her shoulders draped with a dark shawl, an old, slightly built, Indian woman sits in one of the arranged chairs by the side of the altar. The dark skin of her face, tanned to leather-like hardness by the sun and wind, is immutably composed. Only her lips move rapidly in response to the beads of the rosary, which is clutched in her hands.

i

Three matronly women, dressed in bright Sunday clothes, stride to the front of the center aisle. The lace kerchiefs, some white, some black, move with their bobbing heads as they discuss in business-like tones the most advantageous place to sit, kneel, and stand for the next two and a half hours. From their trim, antiseptic appearance and quiet, confidence-exuding air, one would guess that they are summer residents from the United States. Probably they own vacation homes in Cuernavaca, as do many well-to-do families, both from the United States and from Mexico City.

Except for the occasional clatter of heels or the murmur of voices, the soaring interior of the cathedral is filled with silence. The chamber-like quietness is seemingly strengthened by the shaft of dust-speckled light descending from above. Soon the walls will pulsate with the weight of breathing humanity, but for now, stillness reigns.

Like many of the Catholic churches in Mexico, this religious edifice was built by Franciscan missionaries who followed in the footsteps of the Conquistador Cortez after he had succeeded in vanquishing the noble race of Aztecs in 1521. These fervent proselytes fanned out in all directions from Tenochtitlan, the capital of the Aztec empire—over the ruins of which now stands Mexico City—so that even in the remotest villages one may be greeted by the carved wooden portals, worn and faded with age, of a Spanish church built centuries before.

The Cathedral of Cuernavaca, otherwise known as the Church of Our Lady of Assumption, was begun in 1529 with funds provided by the wife of Cortez, and finished in the second half of the century. The design of the church was executed by architects brought from Spain; consequently it was built like a Roman basilica. But many of its features, like the fortress exterior and the murals, recently discovered under a layer of paint, reflect native influence.

In 1952, His Excellency Sergio Mendez Arceo became the seventh bishop of Cuernavaca and immediately launched into a plan to renovate this church, which had been the seat of the diocese since 1891. Most of the notable changes took place inside. The two-decked altar, straddled by Roman columns, gave way to a dais on top of which was erected a simple rectangular altar. High above the new altar, supported by four slender beams, rests a bronze plaque. On the plaque, facing down to the altar, is engraved an open pair of "protective and terrible" hands. Unlike the old altar, which was set aloofly at the very front of the church, the new one faces the people and has been moved forward so that the worshippers may envelop it on either side. Behind the altar, set on an even higher dais—reminiscent of the stone temples built by the Mexican Indians hundreds of years ago—rests the seat from which the bishop preaches to his congregation. The columned side altars, which formerly took up so much room, were torn down to leave the gaunt walls appareled only with black, scythe-like iron candleholders and twelve stone crosses symbolic of the twelve apostles.

One statue, depicting the Virgin Mary ascending into heaven, remains in the otherwise icon-free interior. Finally, two soaring columns, topped by the magnificent Roman arch, still stand at the transept. Paradoxically, this backbone of the church, which has stood for more than four hundred years, is mute evidence of the changes that took place. Look, the columns and arch seem to say, the pomp is gone; the paint, the gilded designs, the frills are gone. They have been replaced by simplicity and dignity. It is a church gone back to the people.

And the people have responded. Every Sunday the men, dressed in slacks and open-necked shirts, and the women, wearing plain cotton dresses and sometimes shawls, inundate the interior until the overflow spills out of the portals into the courtyard. But, above all, the parishioners are drawn by the new phenomenon in Catholic Mexico: "the *Misa Panamericana*," popularly known as the Mariachi Mass.

Now the cathedral is filled. The pews were taken long ago and the people sit on the chairs lining the walls, stand in the back and in the main aisle, and squeeze to the very front, which had been set aside for receivers of communion. People fidgeting with camera equipment and craning their necks, eager for the Mass to begin, also occupy the two balconies at the transept and the choir loft.

Dressed in flashy *charro* costumes, the Macias brothers, one by one, make their way through the crowd. With them they bring guitars, violins, trumpets, a harp, and a bass, along with the traditional instruments of the Mexican Indians: the *maracas*, the *tumba*, the *vihuela*, and the *güiro*; instruments with which, only the night before, they played at the Casino de la Selva night club, or at a party, or at a wedding reception; instruments which, before the advent of the Mariachi Mass, had never been sounded within the hallow confines of a Christian place of worship.

The mariachis stand in their reserved place at the very front of the center aisle, facing the altar. When the *Misa Panamericana* was first performed at the cathedral, the well-known group from Cuernavaca played from one of the balconies at the transept, but as time went by they, like the church itself, descended to be among the people.

At precisely eleven o'clock, the bishop, preceded by his co-celebrants, enters the church in a procession. Holding the stylized shepherd's crook, he walks down the center aisle toward the altar, leading the congregation in a communal Act of Purification. Seconds after the first moment of silence, the chords of the "Angelus"electrifies the throng. The soloist sings and at the *estribillo* (the chorus) the people, two thousand strong, raise their voices in openhearted participation.

Barely does the "Angelus" end when the *tumba* begins to beat out the rhythm of "Señor, Ten Piedad" ("Lord, Have Mercy"). The soloist and the congregation swap line for line and the walls of the lofty Cathedral resound with the celebration of the Mass.

In Mexico, the Catholic Church, which had in the past amassed land and riches while the people starved, was often referred to with fashionable cynicism. That makes the people's lusty participation in the celebration of the Eucharist a phenomenon. Churches were traditionally filled with women and children, but men and college students have begun to speak of the Mariachi Mass with unabashed enthusiasm.

"It's 100 percent *macho*," says a middle-aged lawyer. "I guess in English you'd call it he-man. We Mexican males have had to live for centuries with a thing we call 'black lace mantilla' Catholicism! Of course, those of us who know our faith well enough continued to go to the Mass, but ever since my childhood it's been a kind of private domain for the ladies. We had to sing raggy Porfirian hymns. You Americans would say Victorian. They suited mother to a T, but we men and boys felt like fools. Mariachi music, on the other hand, has always been a man's music. Any Mexican male is proud to listen to it and sing along with it, even though the words are really sacred, as they are in this Mass."[1]

The broad foundation for change and innovation in the Catholic Church was laid by Pope John XXIII and his successor, Pope Paul

---

[1] Diana Serra Cary, "Mariachi: A New Sound at Mass" (Cuernavaca, Mexico).

VI, who, together, guided the first ecumenical council in more than a hundred years. The strict rules of liturgy were liberalized to allow masses, heretofore spoken only in Latin, to be performed in the native idiom of the country. Young musicians in Latin America, inspired by the spirit of change, began to compose sacred music. They were tired of hearing polyphonic Gregorian chant written by European composers centuries before.

Originally, that type of music may have had cultural meaning, but over the years it became so stylized and so aesthetic that it lost touch with the people.[2] Composers such as Delfino Madrigal, who wrote the *Misa Mexicana*; Vicente Bianchi, composer of *Misa a la Chilena*; Rafael Carrion, from whose *Misa en Mexico* are used two hymns in the Mariachi Mass; and J. A. de Souza of Brazil were tired of hearing a quintet chorus singing a Palestrina Mass. In Latin America, especially in Mexico, which has had an inferiority complex in the shadow of its giant neighbor to the north, the authors searched for national character, a self-identity.

Interestingly enough, the direct spark for the Mariachi Mass came from a young French Canadian, John Mark Le Clerk. A pianist, organist, singer, and musician in general, John studied in Canada and the United States before coming to Cuernavaca, where he enrolled at an independent institution known as the Center of Intercultural Formation. The Center was initiated to prepare technical assistance personnel, such as teachers, nurses, technicians, social workers, and missionaries assigned to Latin America[3]. Later the facilities of its Language School were expanded to accommodate business personnel, Latin American research

---

[2] Enrique Medina, Author's interview with him on August 9, 1967.
[3] CIDOC, "Institute for Contemporary Latin American Studies";
CIF Language School; Apdo. 479 (Cuernavaca, Mexico), p. 1.1

specialists, Spanish teachers in US schools and colleges, and university students.

The outspoken Monsignor Ivan Illytch, who is executive director of the Center of Intercultural Formation, as well as of Centro Intercultural de Documentación, which seeks to study the "why" of Latin American problems and documents religious, social, and political trends and movements,[4] and which also sponsors the famed Institute for Contemporary Latin American Studies, appointed John Mark Le Clerc head of a nonexistent music department and asked him to "give serious thought to liturgical music."[5]

Listening to records of the new sacred music—none of which had ever been performed in church—or intended to be used that way—John decided that the best pieces from these compositions could be combined into a Mass that would be representative of all Latin America. Taking language teachers and secretaries from the staff of the Center, the young Canadian formed a choir that sang the *Misa Panamericana* in September 1965 at the Chapel of the Center in Hotel Chula Vista. Bishop Sergio Mendez Arceo, always open to new ideas, attended the Mass and found the music delightful. Subsequently, His Excellency brought fifteen priests, musical experts, and the liturgical committee for the diocese to listen and to give their opinion. According to Carol Holgern, head of public relations of the Center of Intercultural Formation, there were votes for and against the new Mass, but those who favored it did so for specific reasons, while those who opposed it did so on general grounds.[6]

---

[4] Ibid., p. 40.
[5] Cary, "Mariachi: A New Sound at Mass," p. 2.
[6] Holgern, Carol. (Author's interview with her on August 2, 1967).

For this reason, the reaction from Bishop Arceo was favorable, but John Mark Le Clerc came up with an even more daring idea. Why not, he thought, have the *Misa Panamericana* performed by a group of mariachis. This was a radical idea, indeed. To bring into church the mariachis, the same who play in *pachangas* or *cantinas*—the American equivalent of bars—the same who stroll the squares at night in search of sentimental celebrants at sidewalk cafes, seemed nothing less than desecration.

But the daring John Le Clerc was undaunted. The mariachis, he felt, are a genuine cultural outgrowth of the people. They began, in fact, in the time of Emperor Maximilian, who reigned from 1863-1867 before being executed in front of a firing squad on the order of Benito Juarez, the two-time, Indian-born president of Mexico. The Austrian-born emperor brought in musicians from France who played mainly at marriage ceremonies and other festive occasions, which earned them the French label of "marriage" musicians.[7] After the disintegration of Maximilian's court, the idea of the "mariachi" violinists and guitarists was assimilated by the people, who added trumpets and native instruments like the *tumba*, the Indians' harp, and the *güiro*.

Eventually, the music became associated with the *charros,* who are expert horsemen with a reputation for being lady-killers. Soon the "rhythm of every song became the simulated beat of a galloping horse's hooves."[8]

The Center's young head of the music department approached the Macias brothers of Cuernavaca and made the proposition. They were astonished at the suggestion, but agreed, and soon the rehearsals began. They arranged many of the numbers by ear from the records. John Le

---

[7] Cary, "Mariachi: A New Sound at Mass," p. 3.

[8] Ibid., p. 3.

Clerc wrote and arranged others on score sheets. On January 3, 1966, on the occasion of a Nuptial Mass for two staff members of the Center, the mariachis played in church for the first time. The first Sunday after Easter of the same year, Bishop Sergio Mendez Arceo concelebrated the *Misa Panamericana* in the Cathedral of Cuernavaca.

Now the bishop and his concelebrants exchange *el abrazo de paz* (the embrace of peace) and then fan out throughout the entire congregation, embracing the people and saying, *la paz sea contigo* (peace be with you). The people answer, y *tambien contigo* (and with you also) and pass the embrace to their neighbors, who usually are complete strangers. The church becomes alive with motion and conviviality. There is a new feeling of good will that is contagious. Enrique Medina, the seminarian music student who directs the people during the Mass, tells of a woman who came to Mass early in order to reserve a few seats exclusively for her family, but a man who came in later saw the unoccupied space and sat down next to her. The woman protested, but the man answered curtly: "Here, no one has privileges; we are all equal." When it came time for *el abrazo de paz*, their animosity fell and they embraced.[9]

Next comes the distribution of communion and the people, struggling to get to the front, burst out into the hymn "El Peregrino de Emaus." Judging by the sound of the response, it is their undisputed favorite:

> *Por la calzada de Emaus*
> *Un peregrino iba conmigo.*

---

[9] Medina interview.

No le conocí al caminar,
Ahora si, en la fraccion del pan.[10]

On the road to Emmaus
A pilgrim walked with me.
I did not recognize him on the way,
But now, yes, in the breaking of the bread.

Response to the Mass at large has been mixed. At worst, it has been called a "shocking psychological swirl,"[11] but the most typical reaction is one of doubt eventually turning to enthusiasm.

"When people first saw us in church," said Cecilio Macias, the leader of the mariachi group, "they were scandalized because they thought that we would play something like *"La Negra,"* which is the mariachi hymn, but after they heard us, skepticism turned to enthusiasm."[12]

Criticism has been leveled at the fact that the principal hymns of the Mariachi Mass are not even liturgical, that is, not written to be performed in a Mass. But Victor M. Nazario in his *"A propósito de la misa con Mariachi,"* writes: "The rhythms and musical expressions of a people ought to form the base for producing a liturgical music..."[13] "More important than the words are the gestures, the signs, the exclamations, the music, the song, and the whole gamut of the language which a people

---

[10] Publication of the Diocese of Cuernavaca: A song sheet entitled *"Misa Panamericana."*

[11] *The News* (of Mexico City) February 9, 1967.

[12] Macias, Cecilio. (Author's interview with him on August 8, 1967).

[13] Nazario, Victor M. *"A proposito de la misa con Mariachis" Correo del Sur*, 66.06.05, p. 9. John Mark Le Clerc, "Misas Tepotztlan," Publication of Centro Intercultural de Documentación, Sondeos #16, p. 8.

is accustomed to use in expressing their joy at a Celebration (of the Mass)."[14]

Enrique Medina, the seminary student of music, explains: "In selecting music for the Mass we try to find hymns that are simple and easily sung by the people; but at the same time we demand that it have aesthetic integrity."[15]

In the CIDOC publication *Misa Tepotzlan*, John Mark Le Clerc explains that while the Gregorian chant is "asexual," *Senor Ten Piedad* is "music with backbone, with meat." Yet, he goes on to say, "It creates an atmosphere of holiness."[16]

As for the criticism that the mariachis don't belong in church, Victor M. Nazario states: "We must understand that the principal function of the liturgy is to give Christian feeling to life."[17] Seminarian Medina amplifies the idea: "When a man goes to a *Cantina* or a *Pachanga* where the Mariachis play, he enjoys himself and associates his enjoyment with the music. When he goes to church his feeling are entirely different. He leads a double life, so to speak. By bringing the Mariachis to church we are attempting to destroy this duality. We want him to be a Christian all the time. When he goes to the *Cantina* after having heard the Mariachis play in his place of worship, will he act and feel the same as before?"[18]

Finally the hour-and-a-half Mass is over and the bishop, instead of retreating to the sacristy behind the altar, leads the streaming people into the sunny courtyard where he will chat with them, receive their

---

[14] Le Clerc, p. 7.

[15] Medina.

[16] Le Clerc, p. 10.

[17] Le Clerc, p. 8.

[18] Medina.

congratulations, and give special blessings. Instead of being an austere, aloof figure, he is now their father.

Beyond all explanations, praises, or criticisms, one fact remains indisputably true: the *Misa Mariachi* at the Cathedral of Cuernavaca communicates with the people.

BIBLIOGRAPHY

Arceo, Sergio Mendez. *"Reacondicionamiento de la Catedrál de Cuernavaca."* Cuernavaca, Mexico: Diocese of Cuernavaca.

CIDOC. "Institute for Contemporary Latin American Studies: CIF Language School." APDO. 479. Cuernavaca, Mexico.

Cary, Diana Serra: "Mariachi: A New Sound at Mass," publisher unknown; possibly the Diocese of Cuernavaca.

Interviews: Holgern, Carol (August 2, 1967)
                Macias, Cecilio (August 7, 1967)
                Medina, Enrique (August 9, 1967)

Le Clerc, John Mark. *"Misa Tepozteca."* CIDOC, Sondeos #6.

"*Misa Panamericana.*" A song sheet. Cuernavaca, Mexico: The Diocese of Cuernavaca.

The News, Mexico City, February 9, 1967.

BIG SKY COUNTRY

By Tony Mankus

Out here in Big Sky Country, the men wear Levis and smoke Marlboros and sit on wooden fences gazing at the panorama of snow-capped mountains and rolling plains; and they talk of calves and castration and of the man who met his death at Immigrants' Gulch. The wooden bridge, its thick front boards ripped loose, its sides splintered by the straight path of the bulldozer, speaks mutely of the unknown determination of a man who drove it till the tapering dirt path along the side of the mountain disappeared, taking the man and his machine into the rapid stream below. The cat still lays there, its threads exposed incongruously above the rushing water that bubbles angrily around giant boulders and sudden turns, and they wonder why he drove there at all.

And they talk of wheat and alfalfa, of strip farming and stacking hay, and of the fire that desolated twelve hundred acres of forest before the final embers glowed and died. It started in Dead Man's Canyon and swept on, fueled by the wind and the dry underbrush, to the ranch of

Matovich, where men who had come from Columbus, Reedpoint, and Big Timber clustered about their pickup trucks, jeeps, and earthmovers, watching silently as tree after tree crowned into soaring flames.

Out here in Big Sky Country, a man can lie at night under the open sky and listen to the interminable rushing of a stream that, at a distance, sounds like the whooshing of the Southeast wind sweeping across the plains; and he can fall asleep with ease because he doesn't have to lie in a roach-infested bed, and he doesn't have to listen to the cries of the discontent. It's almost easy to feel the spirit that drove a man west and to understand the determination of Conservatism, because even in tragedy a man has dignity here; he doesn't have to wash away in the human cesspool of a big city slum.

June, 1968
Bozeman, Montana

MUISNE

(A Site Report for Peace Corps)

By Tony Mankus

Muisne is an island, but just barely so. It is separated from the mainland only by a river, the Rio Muisne, but for all practical purposes, it might as well be the Galapagos. The only way to get there is by one of several boats that leave the coastal town of Esmeraldas several times a week. Unless you're prepared to take the same boat back the following day, you'd better count on staying there three or four days.

The boat ride is by open sea to avoid the breakers, though it's never so far out that sight of the shoreline is lost. A road connecting Esmeraldas to Muisne apparently has been built, but it is usable only during the summer, the dryer part of the year. The rest of the year, it's flooded and impassable.

The island itself is eleven kilometers long and about two kilometers wide. Most of the population, now down to 2,321 people, lives in the city proper on the northern tip of the island. The houses are made mostly of bamboo, though some are constructed of wood or cement. The attractive new hospital is an example of the latter, though it is yet to be occupied by even one nurse. There's talk of putting the town's private practitioner in charge, but that, as well as the future of the hospital, remains in doubt. The Ecuadoran government is not providing any money to staff it and there is certainly no money in Muisne.

The hospital was built in better days, when banana was king in Ecuador. It used to sell at anywhere from fifteen to twenty-five *sucres* (about a dollar) a case. Now they are giving the fruit away. To be generous, you pay two *reales* (a fraction of a penny) for a bunch of six or eight bananas.

Though all Ecuador was hit hard by the competition in Central America, Muisne got it among the worst. That was all they grew on the island until several years ago. When the competition began to be felt, Muisne was among the first to be pinched. It's far away from everything and the farmers weren't organized. Every banana grower, none very large, was out for himself and, as long as the going was good, nobody wanted to rock the boat. Now all that has changed. Belatedly, a group of banana growers has formed into a co-op, the *Cooperativa Rio Muisne*, which sells to exporter Donato A. Yanuzzelli. Where before they could hardly sell a *racimo* (bunch) for one *sucre* (five cents), they now get 11.5 *sucres* per case (fifty cents).

But that's misleading. On the average, only fifty of the 200 farmers in the co-op get a chance to fill a quota of 500 cases, even though those fifty alone could sell much more. And they sell only once a month, whereas before, they used to load up four or five boats that came every week.

A few of the well-to-do residents who own cattle have managed to survive the crises without being hurt too badly. One of them, Ulvio

Zambrano, claims to own five hundred head of cattle and eight hundred hectares of pasture, though other people say he owns much more.

He drives around in a white Land Rover, one of the two or three vehicles on the entire island. Every morning, when the tide is low, he drives over the seven kilometers of the beach toward the southern tip of the island. There he waits for the huge, leaf-wrapped chunks of cheese that one of his workers delivers on mule-back from the other side of the bay. Usually there are a number of people, such as shoppers and mothers with sick children, who have crossed the bay by canoe to await his arrival for the ride into town.

Ulvio Zambrano is the vice president of the *Asociación de Ganaderos* (The Cattle Association), but like virtually all the organizations in town, it exists in name only. There is an office of *Centro Agricola* (Agricultural Center), but its doors are always closed. The office of *Extension Agricola* (Agricultural Extension), mainly concerned with the control of the coconut palm disease called *Gualpa*, does function, but very often the extensionist, Victor Guerra, has no gas for the outboard motor of his launch. He's supposed to get a fifty-gallon barrel of gasoline from Esmeraldas every week, but the last two times that the barrel was sent out for refilling, it was returned empty. Also, the government is two months behind in paying his salary.

There is no industry in town other than a saw mill, a rice mill, and a mechanic shop—if these can be called "industry." The one bank in town is a branch of the Banco Nacional de Fomento, but it doesn't have full branch status. As manager Pedro Pacheco explained, "Any loan application must be sent for approval to Esmeraldas where it sits on a desk for several months or more and often returns after the crop is near harvest. Sometimes a loan applicant borrows money from a friend to make a trip to Esmeraldas to see if he could speed up the processing, only to return empty-handed and deeper in debt than before."

Besides the red tape, the bank is not willing to give loans for banana cultivation at this time. And if a farmer wants to diversify to other crops—which would be wise—he's got no collateral for a loan. The land sells for about 400 *sucres* (twenty dollars) a hectare and to plant a hectare of rice, let's say, would require an initial investment of 10,000 *sucres* (five hundred dollars), or more.

The tragedy is that there is a lot of rain and the land is as abundant as it is fertile. One afternoon we filled up the gas tank of the extensionist's launch and rode up the Rio Muisne to San Gregorio. Mariano Yepez, a town merchant and a friend of Victor Guerra, the extensionist, took me to some high ground just outside of town and explained:

"This is San Gregorio. As you can see it's a pretty shabby town. It's made up of about a hundred bamboo houses, and even of those few there are many vacant. Some were abandoned before they were even completed. The banana-packing plant you see over there is idle now all the time.

"We are poor," he went on, "but we don't starve, so we're not asking for any handouts. There are fish in the river and when the tide rises, this marsh here beside us gets filled with crabs that can be caught with your bare hands.

"Further up the river there is beautiful virgin land. Some of it has been cultivated by farmers who simply went over there and planted crops without bothering to tell the government about it, but the majority of it just lays there because no one has money to invest.

"As for the future, well, we don't think much about it. There is talk of a road being built up to San Gregorio, but that's only talk. Right now we don't need more talk; we need men who would show us how to grow our crops and how to better the breed of our cattle and pigs. Go back to your country and tell the people that there is a Muisne and a San Gregorio and tell them what it's like over here."

Padre Luis de Giorgi, an Italian of the Misión Camboniana, runs the parish with two assistants, another *padre* and a *hermano*. He talked wistfully of industry coming to Muisne.

"Some of the coconut which is grown on the island," he speculated, "is taken to Manta for vegetable-oil extraction. This could be done right here in Muisne to the general betterment of the whole town, especially in terms of employment. Another possibility is the construction of a plant that would make banana puree, which could be canned and exported. But these are just ideas that have no chance of fruition. The local men who have capital are not willing to invest it in such ventures."

So Muisne remains a sleepy little town. The men stand around in groups at the intersection of the two main streets, talking about the little events of the day. José, one of the few young men in Muisne who hasn't left, is the town errand boy. He meets the boats as they come in, carries luggage for passengers, or shows them to the *barrio* San Pedro, which swings at night with music, booze, and young prostitutes. During the day, the prostitutes lounge around in their sleeping gowns on the front steps of a grocery store, across the street from the nightclub, completely a part of the community, which accepts them without passing judgment.

Perhaps symbolic of this tragic demise of Muisne is its magnificent beach, an untapped natural resource that stretches for seven kilometers in an unbroken curve. The sand is packed so hard that even a fully grown man walking on its surface leaves no tracks. There are no pebbles, even. The only thing that breaks the flat expanse of sand fading into the distant fog is the row of coconut palm trees swaying in unison to the breeze.

Someday it may become a resort area, but for the time being it waits patiently, like the patient women who come there to gather pieces of driftwood that have washed up on the shore.

But there are some faint stirrings of change. In the last several years, the farmers have begun to convert from banana to other crops such as rice, citrus fruit, coffee, and cacao. The coconut palm trees have always been around and the disease *Gualpa* has been pretty much controlled, though there are signs of a new plague, the *Ceridera,* for which no cure has yet been developed. There are wood trees, *Mangre, Guayacan,* and others, and there are pigs and cattle; but for all these things, there is a need for technical assistance and development capital.

Malaria has been virtually eradicated. The campaign is well financed and the head of the malaria campaign in the area, Manuel F. Feijoo, has thorough knowledge of the disease. His statistics are complete and he has maps of even the smallest villages in the county. He has a number of small boats and three outboard motors to transport the field men to even the farthest reaches of the county. In addition to the travel by boat, sometimes these trips take three more days of journey by canoe and by foot.

There is a newly constructed water-purifying plant and a number of wells, as well as electricity and schools. There are a number of primary schools—both public and parochial—and one high school.

But here again there is no cause for optimism. Whether the water is drinkable without boiling is doubtful; the electricity is on only part of the time (6:00 to 12:00 p.m. every night except Saturdays, when it's on from 6:00 p.m. to 2:00 a.m.); and the schools are always short of money. When we were there, the high school teachers were on strike because their pay was two months behind. The question for Peace Corps, then, is whether to send a volunteer to Muisne.

The answer, frankly, would have to be "no."

That there are needs and potential for development in the Muisne area is beyond doubt. But whether a volunteer could fulfill those needs or even begin to develop the potential is, at best, dubious. The people we talked to expressed a desire for a volunteer and even offered assistance and specific proposals for work. Victor Guerra, the agricultural extensionist, suggested that an agricultural volunteer could start a 4H Club and help him in extension work. He offered to put up the volunteer in his large house in the *barrio* of San Pedro. Padre Luis likewise offered lodging and suggested that the volunteer might teach English in his school, which is short of teachers due to the difficulty in meeting the payroll. Manuel Feijoo, the director of the malaria campaign, offered to help in whatever way he was capable, including river transportation. The town council expressed that they wanted to see a volunteer in the municipality. A farmer from San Gregorio expressed that a volunteer might start a credit co-op, which he felt was a real necessity in the area.

Yet it is doubtful that a volunteer could even begin to scratch at the mountain of inertia, the broken spirit of the people that has left them resigned, distrustful, and even cynical. When they open up like the young merchant from San Gregorio did, the people reveal a deep well of hope; yet whether a volunteer, a *gringo*, could shape this innate faith in the future into co-ops, clubs, and fields of rice is questionable. In the four days we were there, we saw barely one game of soccer, a refuge of even the poorest *campesinos* (country dwellers). And when the sun sets over the three or four streets of Muisne, a volunteer feels very alone.

July 24, 1969
Quito, Ecuador

xxiii

The Mankus family; Thanksgiving, 2012
Left to right: Margarita Marchan-Mankus; Camille; Clarissa;
author; Ariana; Margarita

ABOUT THE AUTHOR

Tony Mankus is an attorney and principal with the law firm Mankus & Marchan, Ltd., of Lisle, Illinois, a suburb of Chicago. The focus of his practice is on IRS tax controversies and bankruptcies. The other principal of the law firm is his wife, Margarita Marchan-Mankus, who focuses on Social Security disability issues and real estate matters out of the law firm's office in Aurora, Illinois.

They have four adult daughters: Clarissa, an executive with an insurance company in Milwaukee; Camille, a graphic designer in Chicago; Margarita, third-year medical student in Puerto Rico; and "baby" Ariana, a "firstie" (senior) cadet in the U.S. Military Academy at West Point.

Tony's literary background includes writing and publishing (in various legal journals) a number of technical articles dealing with tax and bankruptcy issues. He has also written more personal and creative articles that were published in "Lithuanian Heritage Magazine" and "Rivulets," a publication of the Naperville Writers Group. Years ago, when he was a Peace Corps volunteer in Ecuador, he also edited a bilingual magazine called "El Ecuador."

Time permitting, Tony is currently working on a novel.